FACING 50

...A VIEW FROM
THE MOUNTAINTOP

FACING 50

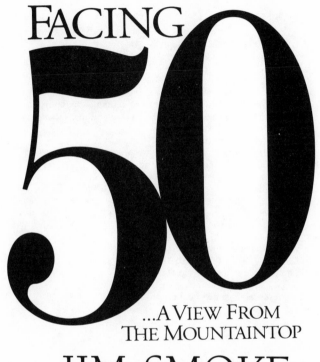

...A VIEW FROM
THE MOUNTAINTOP

JIM SMOKE

THOMAS NELSON PUBLISHERS
Nashville

If you've enjoyed this book or would like information about seminars please write:
Jim Smoke
Box 24450
Tempe, AZ 85285

Published in association with the literary agency of Alive Communications, P.O. Box 49068, Colorado Springs, Colorado 80949.

Published in Nashville, Tennessee, by Thomas Nelson, Inc., and distributed in Canada by Lawson Falle, Ltd., Cambridge, Ontario.

Except where indicated, Scripture quotations are from the NEW REVISED STANDARD VERSION of the Bible. Copyright © by the Division of Christian Education of the National Council of the Churches of Christ in the United States. Published by Thomas Nelson, Inc., Nashville, Tennessee.

Scripture quotations indicated NKJV are from THE NEW KING JAMES VERSION of the Bible. Copyright 1979, 1980, 1982, Thomas Nelson, Inc., Publishers. Quotations indicated KJV are from the King James Version.

Library of Congress Cataloging-in-Publication Data

Smoke, Jim.
    Facing 50 / Jim Smoke.
      p. cm.
    ISBN 0-8407-7745-0
    1. Middle age. 2. Aging. I. Title. II. Title: Facing fifty
HQ1059.4.S56   1993
305.24'4—dc20   93-41879
                                          CIP

Printed in the United States of America.

1   2   3   4   5   6   7   —   98   97   96   95   94

Contents

To Marie, Stan, Verna, Marg, Ruth, and Jean, most of whom are fifty-something and all of whom are my cousins in the Smoke clan.

To Lorraine Hansen, a special fifty-something cousin whose life exemplifies what caring and love are all about.

Acknowledgements

SPECIAL THANKS to all the fifty-something people who contributed to this book in so many ways. No book is a singular effort but a mosaic that blends the input of thousands of fellow travelers.

I owe a great debt of gratitude to my wife, Carol, for all the proofreading, typing, and critiquing.

My friend Jim Davis was instrumental in helping create many of the interactive devices that will make this book an effective guide for personal growth. He is also a sojourner on the fifty-something trail.

To Fritz Ridenour I will always be grateful for his friendship, wistful insights, writer's expertise, and personal affirmation in my writings of this and other books.

Finally, thanks to Rick Christian, my literary agent, for his ability to encourage, affirm, and navigate the rapids of book publishing. Also to Janet Thoma, my editor, and Sue Ann Jones, my copyeditor, who know how to perform surgery on a manuscript and make it whole.

1

The Fifty-Something Dilemma

The fact of aging seems to be one of life's great surprises, a surprise that is most fully sprung in the fifties.

David A. Karp

I REMEMBER MY fiftieth birthday party. If my fortieth was an "over the hill" experience, my fiftieth was an "over the mountain and gone from view" event! My friends wrapped a shawl around me, sat me in a rocking chair, and proceeded to shower me with the gifts one needs to open an infirmary: a big bottle of Geritol, a box of corn plasters, a bottle of hair coloring, a large box of laxatives, and a cane.

Until that moment, I did not feel bad about crossing the great divide between forty-nine and fifty. After all, I still ran several miles a day, played racquetball twice a week, had all my hair, and felt that my body was good for another hundred thousand miles. The only real bump in this passage arrived several weeks later when an application for membership in the American Association of Retired Persons arrived in the mail. The good news was that I had survived for fifty years. The bad news was that I was being pushed prematurely toward the discount heaven of senior citizenry.

After this initial run-in with the fifties culture shock, I steered my body back into the fast lane, bought a new pair of running shoes, headed down the other side of the mountain into the fifty-something years, and forgot about my age. My only reminders occurred when a friend or acquaintance asked, "How does it feel to be fifty?"

I usually replied, "Who's fifty?"

Little did I realize how full of feelings and questions my new decade, the fifty-something years, would be.

The Fifty-Something Years

A few years ago a popular television series, "Thirty-Something," focused on the unique joys and sorrows of the decade between thirty and forty. It chronicled the struggles of appealing characters who left the idealistic twenties to face the realities of the thirties, realizing that life's not always fair and coming to grips with parenthood and marriage. Each week young people turned on the TV and thought, *That's me. That's just what I'm facing.*

The fifty-something years are just as unique, yet they are the least written about and researched span of life in American society. For many, fifty-something is the empty corridor between the crises of the forties and the retirement room of the sixties. For others, it's a ten-year holding pattern, a caution light before the stop sign of retirement.

For those who live these years most successfully, the fifties is a dynamic decade, a prime time of adventure, when more choices about lifestyle present themselves than in any other time of life. One fifty-something woman spoke for many when she said, "This is the happiest and busiest time of my life."

But this kind of dynamic living doesn't just happen. The greatest temptations for us during these years are to consider only the problems that are inherently linked with the fifties and to believe those voices that scream that we are over the hill. For example, people in their fifties have been called the "sandwich generation" because they are often squeezed between the demands of children and those of older parents and relatives. Vocationally, the fifties generation is rapidly becoming the one that is most frequently displaced by loss of jobs and vocations. Sadly, the terms *middle age, middle management,* and *unemployed* are often synonymous during this decade. But the end of a career doesn't have to mean the end to living happily, as we will see in the pages ahead. Many options are available, and sometimes they push a fifty-something person into successful work or a happier lifestyle that exposes the job loss as a blessing in disguise.

For me the fifty-something years seemed to be the "I hope and I need" passage.

The "I Hope and I Need" Passage

In her book *Passages,* Gail Sheehy suggested that the twenties is the "I should generation," the thirties is the "I want generation," and the forties is the "I must generation." Reflecting back on my eight years since reaching the half-century mark, I would suggest that the fifties be called the "I hope and I need generation."

The "I hope" is expressed as you look back at your journey and hope the decisions you made were the right ones, or at least that the wrong ones work out right. Then you look ahead with hope that everything in the future will work out all right too.

The "I need" part comes from the freedom to finally

express openly what you need to continue, change, or challenge your life. Until now, it probably seemed there was constantly a need, and it was always someone else's. Your children seemed to be continually marching toward you with outstretched arms and open hands, saying, "I need! I need!" Now, for the most part, they're adults able to meet their own needs, and perhaps for the first time as you reach fifty you feel free to focus on yourself and your own needs. But it takes pointed retraining of the brain to say out loud for the first time "I need!" Most of us do not do well at this. We make muffled sounds and hope that someone hears them. The fear of not having our needs met when they are made known sends us scurrying back into old emotional habits.

This change in focus at fifty-something has been obvious to me during the past two years as I have traveled around America collecting information for this book. I have asked hundreds of people in surveys how they feel about living through their fifties. The responses show a decade of people who are best described as "shifting gears." Many talked about slowing down their rapid pace of former years. Others talked about career and geographical options that would open new doors of opportunity for them.

While the opportunity to shift gears may increase during your fifties, it's not always easy to actually make those choices and changes. Some of my personal memories of this decade would best be described as "floating through my fifties." Many of the responsibilities that kept me grounded in my forties were gone. The children were on their own. We had moved to another state, so our former support systems were absent. We were uncertain about career options. The only thing I seemed to identify with were the hot-air balloons floating over our desert landscape every morning. My memories seemed to be in constant conflict with my realities. The words of Carl Jung best described my state of mind:

> We cannot live in the afternoon of life according to the program of life's morning, for what was great in the morning will be little at evening and what in the morning was true, will at evening become a lie. I have given psychological treatment to too many people of advancing years and looked too often into the secret chambers of their souls, not to be moved by this fundamental truth.

The changes of the fifty-something years lead us to face many turning points.

Turning Points at Fifty-Something

Because fifty-something is a time of sorting through choices, shifting gears, and regrouping, it is often as a result a time when we experience a turning point. Turning points may be bold and dramatic or subtle and gentle changes caused by a crisis, a challenge, fear, boredom, the influence of other people, or divine intervention. Many of our survey respondents expressed a fifties tiredness with S.O.S., the same old stuff. Their lives and lifestyles had become predictable, boring, and dissatisfying. They were ready for a turning point, and some of them were hoping retirement would be a way of dealing with the S.O.S. "There has to be more to life than this," they told us.

I have listened to many of my fifty-something friends

say repeatedly, "Money is not enough of a reward for doing what I'm doing. At this point in my life, I need emotional satisfaction that impacts my life as well as the lives of others." In short, they need to feel that what they're doing makes a difference. In their book *Midlife Myths,* Ski Hunter and Martin Sundel state:

> Productivity is essential at any age in our lives— however this does not mean a good job with good pay—it is the power to act in a world and in some way shape and influence one's environment. The precise form it takes is less important than the opportunity to contribute to the well-being of the larger community. To be productive means to express one's talents in ways that contribute to and sustain community life. Finding ways to do that throughout one's lifetime is the challenge of productivity.

An example of this was the fifty-two-year-old man who said he had spent his first half of a century "taking" from life, and now in the second half he desperately wanted to "give something back" in a humanitarian way. He was uncertain where this desire would lead him, but he knew he was standing at a turning point.

Many people share his thoughts, but they still struggle with the choice. They are looking for a more meaningful second half, but logic tells them their hard work in the past has earned them the right to future self-indulgence. Choosing self-sacrifice and a more meaningful existence instead may require much thought and deliberate effort, but the results can be rewarding, as I will show in chapter 9.

I remember a retired man living in Florida telling me he had been "exiled to the golf course" until he died. If one were an avid golfer, that might appear to be more of a joy than a life sentence. As we talked further, though, it became apparent that eighteen holes of golf a day till death did not tally up to a meaningful existence for this man. Having lived in Florida for six years, I came to believe that many of the retired men I met were condemned to the golf courses while the retired women were destined to roam the malls from dawn till dusk. A vast number of these were fifty-something people with many years of productivity left in their lives, but someone had apparently convinced them their turning point had ended at the eighteenth hole or at the checkout counter.

Calling Time-Out at Fifty-Something

Most of us have medical checkups from time to time, but few of us ever have *life* checkups. Our "wake-up call" often comes in the form of a major crisis such as an illness, death, accident, job loss, or family problem. Many of life's turning points are brought about by these unexpected events that force us to make an honest evaluation of our goals and priorities. Something that's vitally important to us—perhaps it's a spouse, our health, or our job— is suddenly taken away or drastically changed, and we find ourselves struggling to rearrange our priorities, reconsidering what's really important in our lives *now*.

If we would take time out for a life review *before* we are forced to endure a crisis, we could greatly reduce the pressures that surround the decisions linked to the turning point. This is true, not just in our fifties, but in any decade of our lives. I suggest that people call time-out in the midst of their everyday lives; this gives them an opportunity to plan for the future before these unexpected events happen.

A Time-Out Review

I have several friends who, as they have passed from one decade to the next, have taken a time-out to ask themselves hard questions and seek input from their best friends. You can do the same thing by taking a time-out right now and responding to these questions:

	Yes	No
1. Does what I do (in any area of my life) cause me more happiness than unhappiness?	____	____
2. Am I making the best use of my gifts, talents, and abilities in what I am so busy doing?	____	____
3. Do I usually say "I should" to the things I am so busy doing?	____	____
4. Would I do some things differently if I knew I could not fail?	____	____
5. Does what I do make any difference in today's world?	____	____
6. Am I doing what I feel God would want me to do if I could ask Him personally?	____	____
7. Do I usually continue to do what is easiest for me?	____	____
8. Am I willing to pay the price to change?	____	____
9. Do I know how to take small time-outs for myself?	____	____

To use these questions in a more direct way, go through the list several times, each time applying the questions to a specific area of your life (your vocation, family, relationships, religious life).

Coaches know the final score is often the direct result of skillfully planned time-outs used to improvise, change the game plan, invent a new tactic, or plan a new defense or offense. The same is true for all of us. *Remember: As long as you can continue calling time-outs, the game of life isn't over!*

A Time-Out to Reevaluate Priorities

When Helen and Ben celebrated their twenty-fifth wedding anniversary, they spent a weekend at a quiet bed-and-breakfast on the coast of Maine. In this peaceful setting, they took a time-out to reevaluate what was really important to them as a couple and as individuals.

"Ben traveled a lot in his business; he was frequently away from home, sometimes for a week or more," Helen recalled later. "So I think we both went into this time-out thinking that the other spouse would say the constant travel was a problem. I thought he would say he was worn out by it, that it was too hard, too stressful; he thought I would say I was lonely when he traveled now that our kids had grown up and left home. I guess for some couples that would have been the case, but when we started honestly talking about our priorities—what we liked and didn't like about our lives—Ben admitted he enjoyed the challenges of traveling. He liked the diversity of his different clients around the country and the changing settings he worked in. And I admitted that although I missed him when he was away I liked being alone. I enjoyed this as a time of independence, and I had developed a strong support system of friends and neighbors; whenever I wanted to, I could be with them when he was away. I also had several volunteer activities that kept me involved in the community."

When Ben died two years later at age fifty-five of a sudden heart attack, Helen was pressured by relatives to "move back home" where the couple had met as childhood sweethearts, where many family members still lived, and where they had spent most of their child-rearing years. At first the suggestion sounded logical.

"But then I remembered that discussion Ben and I had had on our weekend away, and I stayed put," Helen said. "I remembered how important my network of friends here had become to me, and also in a way it helped me cope with Ben's death. Yes, his heart attack had probably been brought on by the very active, high-stress life he lived. But I knew he loved that life; he had told me so when we discussed our priorities. So I didn't feel guilty that he had died prematurely because he worked so hard just to support us financially. Remembering that this lifestyle was his preference didn't take the pain away—and I admit that sometimes a little resentment creeps in—but it helps me accept his death and keeps me from feeling guilty."

Don't wait until you *wear* out to take a *time*-out to evaluate your lifestyle and your priorities. By then you'll be too fatigued, confused, distraught, or depressed to do anything productive—except blame everyone else for your problems.

The secret to evaluating your priorities "is to connect with what you care about most deeply," suggests an article in the May 1993 issue of *Prevention* magazine. The article quotes San Francisco psychologist Ross Goldstein, who says, "You must look at what matters to you, what your values are, and how those values might have changed over the years."[1]

These are not easy questions to answer. They need to be wrestled with and faced honestly if they are to be helpful. And when you figure out what's important to you, don't keep it to yourself. Share it; live it out. Make a fresh start. As writer Malcolm Boyd suggests, "The key is: Move outside your stifling, ingrown, self-centered emotional ghetto. Share your feelings with someone else—a friend or counselor. Start to interact in positive ways with other men and women who are richly involved in life."[2]

In the coming chapters we are going to look at the natural turning points of the fifty-something years: the changes in our marriages, our individual lives as men and women, the possibility of early retirement, the added blessing of grandchildren, and the challenge of parenting our parents. We'll also look at the possibility of unexpected difficulties: becoming single again, beginning again when a career ends suddenly, and surviving a midlife crisis. And in each chapter we'll be considering the time-outs, the planning necessary to navigate these turning points successfully.

This book is an attempt to explore the challenges and wonders of the fifty-something decade, to look at creative and successful ways to cope with life's changes, and to make the most of the opportunities that lie ahead.

Chapter

2

How Do You Really Feel about Being Fifty?

Dissatisfaction . . . can happen at any state of life. But in midlife, it typifies the emotional growing pains that nearly everyone feels.

Cathy Perlmutter,
"Self-Help for Midlife Growing Pains,"
Prevention

RECENTLY ON OUR weekly radio talk show in Phoenix called "The Relationship Line," my cohost Pat McMahon and I asked callers to help write this book by telling us how they felt about their fifty-something years. We were inundated with responses for the entire hour, but I was stopped midway through the show by two particular calls. One lady approaching her fifties expressed her feelings in one word: "Fear." This was followed by a gentleman who had been out of work for nine months, had sent out more than 250 résumés and had only seven interviews, and was still jobless. He said he was discouraged but was still out there trying to find work. My emotional and empathetic response as a counselor was to want to make their fear and discouragement go away, but I could not.

Although facing fifty for these two callers was not an altogether happy prospect, they did have one thing in their favor: They were in touch with their inner selves, they recognized their feelings, and they were able to express them to someone else. Maybe, like these callers, you're finding that fifty-something is a time of strong and unexpected emotions.

I am more emotional at fifty-something than at any time since I was a teenager. As a teen, my emotions were tied primarily to the sports I participated in. Today they are tied to almost everything in my life. This does not mean I live every day on an emotional roller coaster. In fact, I stay on a pretty even keel emotionally. What I am aware of is that I feel many things more deeply than ever before, and I know that is directly connected to my heightened sensitivity.

You might think that expressing these emotions would be inappropriate. And certainly some ways of expressing emotions *can be* inappropriate. On the other hand, letting harmful emotions boil and fester inside you, unexpressed, is equally destructive and can have drastic results when they finally are released in an emotional explosion.

It doesn't have to be this way. Emotions are a God-given part of our lives. To deal with them, you must first let yourself feel and acknowledge them. The simple truth is this: *You cannot deal with your feelings until you give them a name.*

Identifying Your Feelings

It is during the fifty-something years that many people discover they have buried their feelings during their first half-century of life. Most of us raced nonstop through our lives without ever taking time to get to know our inner selves. Demands of children, careers, family, and economic survival occupied most of our waking hours and even some of our sleeping time. Our identities were tied largely to what we did vocationally, where we lived geographically, and who we spent our time with socially. Our inner thoughts, feelings, and desires seldom found their way through the jungle of our daily activities to the freedom of open expression. When someone asked how we were doing, we answered with a curt "Fine," or "Tired," or "Busy."

The end result is that we have lost touch with our inner selves and have become one-dimensional persons, emotional robots. In failing to discover and express our inner being, we have lost touch with the part of our lives that helps us know who we really are. If your earlier lifestyle robbed you of your inner identity, the chances are good that some of those around you in your family structure were molded the same way. Psychologists tell us that dysfunctional families are the result of three "don'ts" that take over the family system: *Don't talk, don't trust,* and *don't feel.* These unwritten rules strip those family members of one of their greatest God-given gifts: expression.

In both counseling and seminars I deal with many people who are waking up to the fact that they are not in touch with their thinking, feeling, and acting selves. When I ask them how they feel about certain issues, I often get a blank stare along with a mumbled "OK." Because they never had the freedom to get in touch with their feelings and honestly express them, they now find themselves in a foreign and fearful area.

God created us with the ability to respond to things that happen in our world. To deny this response is to deny our feelings. The four most commonly expressed feelings in all of us, regardless of age, are *mad, sad, glad,* and *scared.* At any given moment, at least one of those feelings is coursing through us. Our very human struggle is to recognize that feeling within ourselves and then express it appropriately. The problem with doing this begins in childhood when we are told that we should have the feelings we describe whenever we tell a parent how we feel. The exception would be if we felt glad or happy, but even then we might have been told that there was nothing to be glad or happy about. So repressing our feelings comes right along with our first tooth and may continue through life until all our teeth fall out.

What feelings are you experiencing during your fifty-something years? I've found it practical to list my current struggles and situations and to identify how I really feel about them. Take a few minutes and list your specific concerns under each general topic in the feelings chart on page 16. Then check the appropriate box to indicate how you feel about each one.

When you complete the chart, you will have a better idea about how you really feel regarding the current issues in your life. Identifying your feelings and expressing them is the first step in resolving them.

If you checked *scared* on the feelings chart, you are experiencing the common fifties emotion of fear. If you checked *mad,* you are feeling another common fifties emotion: anger. Feelings are basically neither right nor

Feelings Chart

Problem or Struggle	GLAD	SAD	MAD	SCARED	OTHER
1. _____					
2. _____					
3. _____					
4. _____					
5. _____					
Relationships: Family/Friends					
1. _____					
2. _____					
3. _____					
4. _____					
5. _____					
Future Events: Plans and Dreams					
1. _____					
2. _____					
3. _____					
4. _____					
5. _____					
Totals					

wrong. They simply are. It is only when a feeling is accompanied by an improper action that we get into trouble. We have a right to feel angry, for instance, but we do not have a right to express it by beating up the person who created the source of our anger.

Let's look more closely at these two common emotions that seem to surge through our fifty-something years.

Fear

As the woman who called our radio show reminded us, fear is a feeling that is common in all of our lives, especially as we think of the possible obstacles that hover over our post-fifty years. We worry about all the unknowns that lie ahead: the fear of not having enough time to accomplish what we want to do; the fear of aging, diminishing health, and mortality; and the unending concern for our children.

Fear of Not Having Enough Time Left

The fear of not having enough time left in life to improve the score is a common dilemma. As behavioral scientist Bernice Neugarten says, "Our life is restructured in terms of time left to live rather than time since birth."

I personally think a lot about the time I have left to live and can readily identify with the cartoon character who opened his fortune cookie only to read "Today is the third day of the rest of your life." No matter how much may be left, you soon realize that the most significant portion is far behind you.

Mountains yet to climb are overshadowed by mountains we wished we had climbed. Dreams that were once alive and obtainable in earlier years now become the empty caverns of our reality. The light at the end of the tunnel appears to be affixed to the train of life that is about to run us down. Time, once unending, now becomes a diminishing resource. To many of the fifty-something generation, the question might be, "Do I have enough money for the time I have left or do I have enough time for the money I have left?"

Fear of Aging, Diminishing Health, and Mortality

The fact of aging seems to be one of life's great surprises. A surprise that is most fully sprung in the fifties. Fears and suspicions of what lies ahead suddenly become of primary interest. Questions about health, career, financial security in retirement, job security, and changing relationships all become more insistent. The basic idea is that you're not as young or old as you feel. It really makes a lot more sense to say you're as young or old as other people make you feel.

My grandson is even troubled by my age. He constantly asks me how old I am. When I tell him, his response is "How old is that?"

I haven't figured out a good answer to his question. I just know that twenty-two million other Americans are also fifty-something.

After the 1990 census, the U.S. Census Bureau informed Americans that our whole culture is getting older; Americans are living longer and we are apparently more healthy in our longevity. The AARP has one of the largest memberships of any group in America today. Its lobbying potential in Washington is second to none. Millions of new members are added each year from the swelling ranks of fifty-something people. One does not have to be retired or even plan to someday be retired in order to join. If you are over fifty, you will probably receive a membership application (as I did), which enables you to join the stampede.

Obviously, fears of health and mortality occupy a lot of our thinking time. Writing in *The Gerontologist* in 1988, David Karp said, "There is a momentum of mortality occurrences in the fifties. People in their fifties find that members of their age . . . begin to die with some regularity, which intensifies one's own recognition that life ends." Faced with the issue of real and imminent mortality, some begin a mad scramble to climb their unclimbed mountains while others seem content to pitch camp at the base and enjoy the view.

One of life's great philosophers and baseball players, Satchel Paige, once said, "How old would you be if you didn't know how old you was?" I've found a lot of comfort in that question.

Concern for Our Children

Concern for our children and other family members appears to reach a peak in our fifties decade. One of my fifty-something friends repeatedly tells his children that his goal is to get to see them become independent *before* he dies because it is for certain they will have to be independent *after* he dies.

We all want our children to be successfully progressing on a life track that increasingly sets us free from worrying about their futures. Discerning parents know that this is more a myth than a reality. Concerned and caring parenting never ends. Our children get divorced. They lose careers. They move to distant states. They remarry and create new blended families. They experience financial loss. And much to some parents' dismay, they may even want to return to our homes with our grandchildren in tow. A recent television talk show interviewed grandparent couples who were now responsible for the custody and raising of their grandchildren, an ominous responsibility that would send most of us moving away and leaving no forwarding address.

Dealing with the Fears of the Fifties

To overcome a fear, you have to acknowledge it and enter a deliberate process to relieve it. Ultimately, you have to fly to remove your fear of flying.

And even when an edge of fear remains, your self-confidence is boosted because you have accepted the challenge. Ask yourself, "What is the worst thing that can happen to me in this fear?" For instance, the answer to one of the fears we've discussed here is, "If I don't have enough time left to do everything I want to do, it just won't get done. Does that really matter? In the long run probably not." Once that part of the problem is identified and conquered, the fear is reduced and can ultimately be removed.

There is an enduring theme throughout Scripture regarding fear. From the beginning of the Bible to the end, the message is "Do not fear!" Why? Because God promises to take care of our fears if we allow Him to take care of our lives. The Bible never says we will not have fears; they are a part of our human condition. But when they invade our lives, we can name them, seek help, and trust God to alleviate them in some way, such as the process outlined in this chapter.

The second most common feeling that surges through the fifty-something years is anger.

Anger

I've worked with many fifty-something people who are walking bundles of anger waiting to explode. They are angry that life has not turned out as they once planned. They are angry at their parents, their spouses, their children, their employers, the government, society, and God. They live defensively in an emotional prison, repeating their "life's not fair" doxology a dozen times every day.

Tom was one of those persons. He tried to ignore the restlessness that crept into his mind as he passed the mid-century mark. Secure in his job, happy in his marriage, Tom told himself, *What more could a man want? I'm healthy. I have a loving wife. I'm financially stable. There's no reason for me to feel discontented. So I won't!*

But the nagging feelings kept pecking away at Tom's spirit while he determinedly tried to ignore them. The fact was that Tom was angry at his younger brother Steve, a man who, in Tom's eyes at least, had lacked direction and bounced aimlessly from one job to another throughout his adult life. As a result he had not come close to acquiring Tom's success in business—or in his personal life, for that matter.

Now divorced and trying to put two sons through college, the younger brother had appealed to his and Tom's parents for financial help, and they had responded as much as they could. When their savings were threatened they had even hinted to Tom that he should offer Steve some financial help too. "After all," they said, "you've been a lot luckier than Steve. You can chip in without even noticing the money's gone. You should share some of your blessings with your brother's sons."

And Tom had.

But he resented doing it. After all, he reasoned, he had been working hard while Steve had been living for the moment, always looking for a career that would bring him happiness instead of a financially stable future. His resentment had grown into anger—which he refused to acknowledge. He was surprised by how strongly he felt about the situation, and he believed it was wrong for him to have these feelings. So the anger smoldered away silently inside him, causing him to gradually withdraw from contact with his brother, his nephews, and his parents. Polite and unruffled on the surface, he made excuses for avoiding seeing them or attending family gatherings. In this self-imposed isolation the anger linked up with guilt—*I shouldn't be angry about helping my nephews through college.* And together those feelings grew until they constantly simmered inside him, a ticking time bomb that would eventually explode in consequences of health problems or total family alienation—or both.

Tom had reason to be angry, but he refused to name that anger and share it with others.

Like the other prevalent fifties emotions, anger must first be named and then shared with others as part of the process of healing. Name your feeling and then claim it.

Sharing Your Fear and Anger

Identifying your jumble of feelings is only the first part of growth in this area. For feelings to be processed, they have to be shared with those you trust. But the tough thing about sharing feelings with another person is that you might want that person to take responsibility for your feelings and try to resolve them for you when what you really need from him or her is simply a listening ear.

That's what happened when Anne confided to her husband that she was filled with unhappiness following her fifty-first birthday. "Somehow, turning fifty wasn't that big a deal," she said later. "It was even kind of fun getting all the attention and the little gag gifts from my friends. But on my next birthday, there was no celebration, no jokes. It was as if the fun part of growing older was behind me and now only the serious stuff was left. I was miserable, and I didn't really know why."

She tried to explain to her husband what she was feeling, but before she'd said two sentences the tears started flowing. Her husband interrupted her and pulled her into his arms. "Don't cry, Honey. You'll be all right," he said. "You're not getting old—after all, you're not as old as I am, and look at me: I'm still going strong. Let's call Bob and Pam and see if they'll meet us at that new French place for dinner tonight. That'll perk you up, huh? And maybe this weekend we can go to that flea market you've been wanting to check out. You just need to stay busy, that's all. Don't think about getting older; it happens to all of us and there's nothing we can do about it, so it's best to ignore it!"

Anne's husband meant well, but his string of clichés and pat responses wasn't what Anne needed most right then. He wasn't *listening* to her. When no one listens to us we shrivel up and die emotionally. This is unfortunate because, for the most part, we live in a speaking world rather than a listening world. Instead of listening we speak.

Effective listening to one another occurs in two ways: with the ears of our head and the ears of our heart. People who are struggling through their feelings make heart sounds, but it takes a perceptive ear to pick up these sounds. That's why good listening is always a delicate endeavor and requires total concentration.

I continue to be amazed at the healing that happens in our work with support groups. Six people sit in a group each week and share their feelings about everything that is going on in their lives. When they leave they feel stronger and closer to the others in their group because they have shared their feelings.

One of the most valid reasons for sharing feelings with others is that it helps you know that you are still normal, healthy, and alive. Everyone needs to be able to say, "I feel all these things and I am still okay." C. S. Lewis once said that we are drawn to each other by these words: "What! You too? I thought I was the only one!"

Fear and anger are common negative feelings of the fifties. However, some emotions of this era can be quite positive—and should be relished and enjoyed.

New Positive Feelings at Fifty-Something

Although many fifty-something people have been robbed of the right to have and express feelings, many others at fifty begin to experience, acknowledge, and live out new feelings that are coming to the fore in their lives.

You may find that some feelings, even though they are positive, display themselves in embarrassing ways and at improper times while other feelings tend to overpower and immobilize you. You can be as uncertain with some feelings at fifty-five as you were with similar feelings at fifteen. In fact, your feelings in the fifties can make you question whether you are on the edge of senility—or moving into new depths of your sanity.

Three of the relatively new feelings I connect with my inner self at fifty-something are feeling more sensitive, more relaxed, and more reflective. They seem to have appeared out of nowhere and taken up residence in my life, and judging from our survey respondents, I am not alone.

Feeling More Sensitive and More Relaxed

It's not that I was insensitive in the first half of my life, but now, along with some of my friends, I confess to being far more sensitive in my second half. I feel for people who are hurting more than ever before. After twenty years in the divorce-recovery field, it is easier to empathize and even cry with them in their grief.

I can also cry more quickly while watching a heart-tugging movie or television show. Some days I think I can even cry at the commercials. It makes me wonder whether I am "losing it" or if I have finally "found it." I want to adopt all the dogs that need good homes. I want to find big brothers and big sisters for kids who need them. I want to coach Little League again and encourage the players rather than yell at their mistakes. I want to go to mission fields and assist those who need help. I want to make famine, violence, and prejudice disappear.

Perhaps this happens because in my fifties I feel more

relaxed. I've slowed down enough to really see for the first time what is going on around me, and I respond to it through my feelings and emotions. Or maybe I'm so overwhelmed by it all that the only fitting response is an emotional and sensitive one. Or maybe it's just that I can finally say, "I really don't care what others think when I express my feelings." It is comforting to have lived long enough to own my inner self and let it appear in public with me more often!

For me, being more sensitive means I really see some things I missed before, and I can fully respond to them in ways I choose. It means I freely open myself up to things that will impact my life, and I no longer live as guarded and carefully as before. Increased sensitivity also means I open wide the door to all my senses and take new risks.

As Helen Hayes pointed out in her book, *Our Best Years,* "The best time to take some daring steps is when you get older. You no longer have to account to a parent; you're not responsible for your children. Why shouldn't you change things if you want to?" She quotes the Reverend William Sloane Coffin, Jr., who said, "Our greatest moral problem today is cowardice." Adds Hayes, "Self-doubt and fear of failure are the leg irons that keep us chained to the wailing wall of *un*accomplishments."

Being sensitive means I'm moving through life with my antennae up rather than down. It allows what once were interruptions to now become opportunities to increase my sensitivity.

Being sensitive means looking beyond the edge of where you are and seeing and responding to others' needs. I believe most of us are sensitive. We have just allowed our sensitivity to be buried under layers of protective coating. Sensitive people get walked on, used, taken advantage of, and laughed at. Sensitivity is looked at as a sign of weakness rather than strength. I love it when important people cry. It lets me know they are really human after all.

Feeling More Reflective

Being reflective means more than having the ability to look back at your life and remember where you came from. It is more than looking through family albums and watching your children grow up through the eyes of Kodak. Being reflective is allowing your memories to influence what you may still become. It is learning from your journey what it will take to complete it. It is knowing what you know without having to tell someone that you know it. It is smiling at those who think they know everything and don't. A reflective person has a gentle sense of security that comes from knowing "this too shall pass." In our fifties the things that once looked like mountains ahead of us now seem more like small hills when viewed through our rearview mirror of life.

At this age we can look at what we have lived through and add up some wins and losses. My reflection has taught me that what I then considered losses were really wins. I have discovered the reverse is also true.

This tallying of wins and losses can be a negative experience if all we're doing is keeping score. But this kind of reflection can also be a source of motivation or a way to ease ourselves into contentment. We have a choice to be reflective with regret or reflective with hope.

I wished for many years that I had earned my Ph.D. by age twenty-eight so I could join a major denomination and work my way up to become senior pastor of a megachurch somewhere in America. By most standards, that would have meant I had won the things I wanted and could rest in my accomplishments. But now as I tally up my wins and losses I see that if I had done that, the chances are I would not have written a best-selling book on divorce recovery, *Growing through Divorce,* nor would I have traveled and ministered in hundreds of churches across America over the past fifteen years. So where did I win and where did I lose?

As I reflect on my first fifty years I sometimes wish I could change many things about my parenting and my being a husband, a friend, and a minister. In reflection my priorities are vastly different than they were in reality. Since I cannot change the yesterday things, I focus instead on passing along what I have learned to those yet to learn. Discovering my inner self allows my reflective self to be fully present in my life. Living with a life of regrets kills the reflective spirit. Living with hope nourishes it.

Reflection also allows me to slow down and not be in a hurry to live. St. Vincent de Paul said, "He who hurries delays the things of God." I believe this is primarily because God is never in a hurry. To hurry is to get ahead of God, and when one is ahead of God, he or she cannot get direction from Him.

Lighten Up!

Recently a ninety-year-old lady in our city skydived from a plane at twelve thousand feet while her circle of friends waited anxiously on the ground. They cheered for her, but none wanted to accompany her. They celebrated her feat, but she was the only one who experienced its emotional thrill. I am sure there were a few of her friends who said those death-defying words, "I wouldn't do that if I were you!" They didn't—and she did! Because they wouldn't take the risk they couldn't fully share her joyful feelings of accomplishment.

Similarly, many people spend a lifetime refusing to risk acknowledging their feelings. As a result they are robbed of the joy that emotional expression can give. As you think about expressing your feelings in the coming week, ask yourself the following questions:

- How many times have you wanted to cry or yell or laugh but did not for fear of what people would think?
- Have you ever wanted to run through a fountain in your business attire?
- Have you ever wanted to dance in the streets like Zorba the Greek?
- Have you ever wanted to come into your office in the morning singing at the top of your lungs?
- Have you ever wanted to visit the cemetery where your parents were buried and tell them that you feel very alone now that they are gone?
- Have you ever wanted to tell your children that you are fearful for their future because of the direction the world is heading?
- Have you ever wanted to tell some people you have never told that you really love them?
- Have you ever wanted to say a loud "Amen" in Sunday worship but realized you were *Presbyterian?*
- Have you ever wanted to roller skate, play marbles, or bring out your yo-yo at work when the boss is trying to be serious?

As you read my short list of emotional expressions, you may want to add a few of your own. My suggestion is to try the ones you feel strongest about.

I would like to do some or all of the above and I would also like to:

_____

_____

_____

_____

When I can freely own and share my emotions, it makes me a more relaxed person. When the things that bubble and gurgle inside me can find release, I can approach life without a tension overload. When I see tense people around me, I want to sing the old Simon and Garfunkel song "Feelin' Groovy" to them. I want them to spend some time "kicking down the cobblestones" instead of kicking the people around them.

Right before I spoke to a group of people recently the host for the evening spent a few minutes talking with me. Her final comment before introducing me was, "How can you be so relaxed before you have to speak?" I could have given her five or six different reasons for my relaxed state; the best one was a comment a friend had told me: "The most important person in the room is the speaker before he or she speaks. The least important person in the room is the speaker after he or she speaks." Understanding the balance between the two should make anyone relaxed. If you really know who you are, you will not take yourself so seriously. If you are not too serious, you will be more relaxed.

Fifty-something is a wonderful time to quit taking

yourself so seriously. It is a time to relax and enjoy some of the credibility you have built over the years. It is a time to strengthen your inner self and allow it to be revealed. There are many fifty-something people who have yet to get in touch with their inner spirits. They continue to search for meaning in life outside themselves. Failing to realize that real happiness is an inside job, they move through their fifties in a state of inner denial. The fifty-something decade has many twists and turns—denied dreams and unfulfilled promises. Question marks at times outnumber exclamation marks. Inner battles are fought along with outer wars. Some people lose themselves in their fifties while others find themselves for the first time. Through it all, our inner selves still struggle to emerge.

Reflect with me for a minute and agree that: Even though I sometimes will get . . .
Sad,
Mad,
Glad, or
Scared . . .
I am becoming more . . .
Sensitive,
Reflective, and
Relaxed!
And I think I like it! It even feels good!

3

Still Married after All These Years

People who have spent a lifetime together see each other not only as they are but also retain an image of how the other looked in the early days, like a double exposure that hides to a large extent the telltale signs of the passage of time.
Olga Knopf, M.D.

THAT MORNING THE woman caller to my radio show, "The Relationship Line," who said her predominant feeling about being fifty-something was fear, also told me she had been married for thirty-five years and did not want a divorce. "But," she said, "I don't know how much longer I can live in this relationship." Communication had long since ceased, she admitted, and most emotional threads had been severed.

She wanted to know: Should she leave the relationship, learn to live with it, or find a way to improve it?

Unfortunately, this kind of appeal for help is becoming more typical of the daily flood of calls to our offices at Growing Free, Incorporated, the umbrella organization that includes the Center for Divorce Recovery. It typifies the state of many fifty-something men and women who are living in lifeless marriages with emotionally brain-dead spouses. They're miserable, but for reasons of economics, security, and companionship they stay in marriages of convenience—until they can no longer stand the zombie-like life they're leading. In private, some of these spouses describe themselves as "serving a sentence called marriage" while outwardly they portray a public facade as the contented crew. On the inside, however, there is a hollow emptiness that only grows larger as the years pass.

These partners are at the extreme opposite pole from those fifty-something couples who are happy, excited, and growing in their long-term marriages.

"It's almost as if we've gotten remarried," one happy fifty-something wife confided. "When we were dating— all those years ago—we kept looking forward to the time when we would be married. We were anxious for it to happen; we dreamed about it and shared those dreams with each other. Then the kids came along and somehow being married, being husband and wife, took second place to being Mom and Dad." Toward the end of those "Mom-and-Dad" years, she said, a new kind of anticipation started growing within her and her husband.

"It happened slowly, now that I think about it. One day my husband looked up from a sports magazine and said, 'Someday I'd like to go fishing in Alaska.' I said, 'Yeah, me too. We'll do it when the kids are gone.' After that, the phrase, 'when the kids are gone,' kept popping up in our conversations. It was like we were back in those days when we had said, 'When we're married we'll do so-and-so.' We started anticipating all the fun things we would do when the kids were out on their own."

And now that the kids *are* gone?

"We still love seeing and hearing from our children, of course," the wife said. "But we're having so much fun together, doing all those things we couldn't do before—

even if it's just dancing in the kitchen without hearing giggles coming from the next room."

Surely most couples want this kind of fifty-something marriage—rewarding, nurturing, growing. But too often their progress is impeded by something much more serious than giggles coming from the next room. For some couples, married happiness is blocked by a mountain of unresolved issues leading all the way back to the childhood of one mate or the other. Dysfunctions that are not resolved are either lived out or passed along to another generation, and it is far more difficult to seek resolution for long-standing struggles in midlife than in earlier years. Long-term habits are hard to break, and the impatience factor increases with age. When all these elements continue to build, unfettered, the marriage gap can widen until divorce or suicide begins to look like the only escape from a desperate existence.

If you sense that your marriage is being damaged or destroyed by unresolved issues from your or your spouse's past, seek out professional help without delay. Exposing and resolving these enduring sources of emotional pain may not be easy, but with help from a caring professional it can be done—and in many cases it can change your life and save your marriage.

Dodging Potholes in the Fifty-Something Marriage

While fifty-something marriages offer opportunities for growing pleasure and intimate companionship, they also must withstand much tension and many changes. Spouses must endure internal and external pressures that affect no other decade of married life. Many long and happy marriages flounder and break up in this sea of

fifty-something turmoil. Those marriages that have already been in conflict for many years may reach the
breaking point with the added load of fifty-something
baggage.

As our marriages move through these potentially
treacherous years, many couples stumble along blindly,
hoping they can avoid the obvious pitfalls—or wondering
how they can get out of the ones they fall into with
increasing frequency.

In an attempt to keep you from breaking a leg or
breaking up your married life, let me suggest ways to
avoid seven of the obvious (and not so obvious) potholes
in your fifty-something journey as husband and wife. By
following these suggestions you may be able to turn these
potential potholes into advantages that can strengthen
and enhance your marriage.

1. The Empty-Nest Syndrome

A great deal of marital energy is exerted in organizing
and balancing the lives of the couple's children. Sometimes it seems every ounce of parents' energy is expended
in meeting children's needs—and too often, their wants
—while the parents' needs go unfulfilled. Parenthood becomes an all-consuming venture with an eventual re-
prieve only dreamed about while waiting in the dentist's
reception room.

Then, as suddenly as they appeared, the children are
gone, the house falls quiet, and the husband and wife
enter a period of withdrawal. Each begins to wonder who
the other is. Without the children as their primary focus
they wonder what they have in common with each other.
In many marriages this occurs during the fifty-something
years, and it becomes a time of reconnecting or discon-

necting. Some parents weather this time period with no ill effects on their personal relationships as husband and wife. Others are distracted, distressed, and destroyed.

As you contemplate your empty nest you need to reassess your new identity. Before your children left home you may have thought of yourself primarily as a parent, then as a spouse, and then as something else—a housewife, an executive, an artist. Although your children are a part of you forever, with the easing of your parental responsibilities, you now may put new emphasis on other relationships and other priorities. The real issues for empty-nesters may become apparent as each of you truthfully answers the three questions that follow. After you record your answers individually, compare your responses and discuss your feelings:

1. Who am I now?

_____

_____

2. Who are you now?

_____

_____

3. Who are we now?

_____

_____

The empty-nest period is a dramatic time of change. Your passage through the empty-nest stage will be filled with many feelings. Joy, sadness, release, freedom, loneliness, and loss of nurturing are only a few. Suddenly you stand again as you stood many years ago at the altar of marriage: alone. Or, in a growing number of blended families today, this may be the first time a husband and wife are really alone together.

The years after the children leave can be a time of long-anticipated togetherness and happiness—or it can be something far less rewarding (if not devastating) as you get to really know each other. Where you go from this point will depend on your ability to regroup and your willingness to assimilate your lives together in new ways. If you have moved together through the previous years of your marriage, your passage through the empty-nest stage will be easier than if you have gradually grown apart. If your children were your only reason to stay married, you will both be frantically searching for a new reason to do so now.

Part of the solution for dealing with the empty-nest syndrome starts by visualizing and talking about what your lives will be like when your children leave *before* they actually depart. Rather than seeing it as a giant release valve from responsibility, try to visualize it as a place of transition for both you and your spouse to reconnect to each other in new ways. Many fifty-something couples view the empty nest as the beginning of the "us" period of their lives when a new closeness between husband and wife begins to grow.

2. Nothing in Common after All These Years

When I talk with people in divorce recovery, I often ask what originally attracted them to their now-departed spouses. Some say they were too young to know. Others state they were looking for someone who had the things they did not have, and still others admit they married someone they thought they could change to be more like themselves. Whatever the reasons, all assure me they were in love at the time.

Popular opinion may state that opposites attract, but reality verifies that couples with nothing in common will not stay together as long as those who share many interests. *Having things in common is really the foundation of a healthy marriage.* "When couples fail to develop a new intimacy in these years, the problem is usually that they find they no longer have any common interests," say William H. Bergquist, Elinor Miller Greenberg, and G. Alan Klaum in their book, *In Our Fifties.* "They discover new time together in their fifties but have nothing to share in that time."[1]

Friendships and identities are linked by the threads of similar experiences and by social events we enjoy sharing with each other. Communication grows stronger when we have things to talk about that are of interest to both of us. Likes and dislikes, hobbies and interests, faith and values, vocations and goals are only a few of the possibilities. In a growing, thriving marriage, a couple's common interests may evolve or change over the years. If you and your spouse share common interests, your enjoyment of those interests can fill in for the loss you're feeling when your children leave home and bring you both a continued sense of comfort, joy, and stimulation. On the other hand, if you enter the fifty-something years with nothing in common, your marriage may soon be invaded by a desperate loneliness.

It takes work to avoid—or crawl out of—this kind of pothole, but it can be done if both spouses are open-minded and willing to try. It took Emily and Paul more

than a year to discover an activity they both enjoyed—
and it came as a surprise to both of them. They had tried
traveling, golfing, antiquing, and going to the symphony.
But they hadn't found anything they both enjoyed
equally.

When their church became involved in a program to
build homes for poor families in their city, Emily and
Paul hadn't noticed. After all, Emily thought of herself as
a homemaker, not a home builder, and Paul often reminded friends that he even hired someone to come each
year to switch the screens on their home with storm windows. "I'm not a do-it-myselfer," he would joke.

But when church friends asked them to help supply a
meal for workers, Emily cooked a ham and Paul agreed to
go with her to deliver it to the inner-city building site.

"The site supervisor mistook us for helpers," Emily
said later with a laugh. "When we got there, she said, 'Are
you with the church group?' and when we said yes, she
directed us to a line of people handing up materials to the
workers on the roof. The next thing we knew, we were
pounding nails and setting up concrete forms for the
sidewalk. And at the end of the day we were sore and
exhausted—and exhilarated. We were hooked."

It may take awhile, but eventually you can find some
enjoyable activity, interest, hobby, or sport to pursue together as Emily and Paul did. Discuss your interests and
find some possibilities. Look for groups or activities listed
in the newspaper. You may have to be willing to try
something new until you discover something you both
enjoy.

Most importantly, remember that what you, as a married couple, have most in common at this point are your
present and your future, barring any unforeseen event.

Use that idea as your starting point and launch your search for common interests.

3. Being Taken for Granted

People in long-term marriages tend to take each other for granted. The most common of the "takens" include:

You will always be here for me.
You will always love me.
You will always be able to provide for me.
You will always be the same.
We will always be together.

Making these assumptions in a marriage is living more in fantasyland than on reality ridge. People who take things for granted are seldom appreciative of the everyday blessings in their lives. After a time, they come to believe life owes them these little gifts. They seldom say thank you for anything.

When you take someone for granted you demean him or her. You send the unspoken message, *You are not worth much to me.* You also rob this person of the gift of human appreciation. And to be loved and appreciated gives all of us a reason to live each day. When that gift is withdrawn or denied over the years, our spirits wither and die. People may endure this hardship and stay married forever, but they are only serving a sentence. In long-term marriages where one or both spouses are continually taken for granted, a wall of indifference arises between husband and wife. The longer the marriage, the higher the wall and the greater the human isolation. The way out of this woodpile is simple but crucial:

- Start saying thank you and showing appreciation for anything and everything.
- Be more consciously tuned in to what is going on around you.
- Become more giving and affirming.
- Specialize in the many little things that mean a lot: Bring each other flowers, take long walks in the country, lie on the floor in front of the fireplace, prepare breakfast in bed for each other, hold hands in public and walk in the rain, send caring and funny cards to each other in the mail, buy each other small gifts for no apparent reason.

Remember: A thirty-five-year marriage does not guarantee year number thirty-six. Take nothing for granted just because you have it today.

4. Double Exposure

The lifeview from fifty-something is both panoramic and narrow, and it's framed by failure, fear, and hope for most couples I have talked with. The panoramic view consists of looking back at the yesterdays in our marriages and deftly picking apart the joys and sorrows, tragedies and triumphs, then filtering them through the hindsight of "shoulda, woulda, and coulda."

There is a strong fascination in looking back at life through this panoramic rearview mirror and either becoming nostalgic or regretful. I have spent some of those moments reflecting on:

- My unfulfilled dreams.
- The relationships I wish I had given better care of.

- The greater schooling I wish I had obtained years ago.
- The better business person I wish I had been.
- The better parent I would like to have been.
- The stronger faith I wish I would have had during times of weakness.

For many of us, our yesterdays can be summed up with the words "if only I had . . ." In many marriages both husband and wife have "if onlys" that need to be equally shared and owned. Instead, many spouses point the finger at each other, castigating and blaming each other for not making dreams come true. In empty moments it is easier to look back in this way than to deal with the present, but it is always unhealthy to try to transfer your failures to someone else.

A healthy marriage relationship at fifty-something involves a mutual ownership in the losses in life as well as the wins. In most people's lives, the losses will always seem greater because we tend to focus on the negatives rather than the positives. What we desperately need is to learn how to celebrate the victories so they are more firmly imprinted on our memories than the losses.

While the panoramic view to the past leads us to say, "if only," our tomorrows can be identified with the question "what if?" The narrow view from fifty-something comes when we look ahead at the remaining years of our marriage and wonder what the future holds for us. As we do so, most of us can acknowledge the fears of the future that gnaw at the edge of our marriage.

We survive on our ability to make changes in our present that will remove some of the fears of any future place we will come to. That's why I like to say the present is the place for the "I can!" Here are a few of the common "I cans!" I have listened to in recent months. Share your response after each statement and add a few of your own at the conclusion.

	Yes	No
1. I can finally put up with my mate's idiosyncrasies.	_____	_____
2. I can accept the fact that we *both* look different than we did thirty years ago.	_____	_____
3. I can accept some of the new eccentricities in my spouse that were not there in prior years.	_____	_____
4. I can accept the fact that we both forget things more frequently than before.	_____	_____
5. I can accept the reality that everyone over fifty needs six pairs of reading glasses and can never find any of them.	_____	_____
6. I can accept the strange, unknown phenomenon that red traffic lights at times appear green to one or both of us.	_____	_____
7. I can accept the fact that every fifty-something woman, including one's wife, needs to be told she looks much younger than fifty-something.	_____	_____

Now it's your turn. You could probably take off from this point and add another fifty or so personal "I cans" to the list!

I can

_____

_____

_____

_____

_____

5. Stagnation or Growth?

What happens in a fifty-something marriage when one person is climbing the mountain of growth and exploration while the other is making a slow descent to the bottom—or never moved from the bottom in the beginning? By fifty-something these spouses certainly will discover how different they are; then they will either ignore each other or follow divergent pathways for the rest of their lives. Marriages stagnate because one or both partners are not growth-oriented.

I'd like to share the short poem, "The Oak and the Rosebush," which I've used in workshops over the years to illustrate differences in growth. Its author is unknown.

An oak tree and a rosebush grew,
Young and green together,
Talking the talk of growing things—
Wind and water and weather.
And while the rosebush sweetly bloomed
The oak tree grew so high
That now it spoke of newer things—
Eagles, mountain peaks, and sky.
"I guess you think you're pretty great,"
The rose was heard to cry,
Screaming as loud as it possibly could
To the treetop in the sky.
"And you have no time for flower talk,
Now that you've grown so tall."

"It's not so much that I've grown," said the tree,
"It's just that you've stayed so small."

We could substitute the words *husband* and *wife* for *oak* and *rosebush*. The great failure in human growth is that we neglect to invite those closest to us to grow along with us—or that we refuse the invitation when it is offered.

Although it can happen to wives, as well, men are often the prime violators in this area. They climb the corporate ladder, leaving the wives at the bottom rung to manage home and family. When the children finally leave home, the wife is left stranded without an identity and purpose while the husband is so far up the ladder that the wife can seldom catch up to him. A man in this position often goes searching for someone closer to his own experience and interest. There are numerous variations on this theme with a wide cast of different characters, but the end result is usually the same: the breakup of a marriage where dual growth was neglected. Many times, one partner will encourage the other to venture into new areas of growth only to be spurned by the other spouse's disinterest or busyness in other areas. After repeated attempts, the growing person slowly moves away and leaves the other to stagnate.

Another variable occurs when one spouse—most often the husband—moves toward the no-growth mode due to retirement or job loss. At this point, the wife, of necessity or design, may choose to accept the challenge of growth by launching a new career or reviving one she started earlier in life. It takes a strong and healthy marital relationship to navigate these rapids of change in marital growth. Due to economic realities in our country, this role reversal is becoming more common. The greatest danger is that the wife meets the challenge to get on with her life, thriving in this new area while the husband opts to sit on the sidelines and watch. There are many ways to prevent stagnation in a fifty-something marriage. Here are a few of them:

1. Take classes that both of you can attend at a local community college.
2. Explore new hobbies that can be shared together.
3. Work together in shared community service projects and church missions.
4. Live overseas for a time in a home-exchange program to add a new dimension to your cultural understanding.

Now add some ideas of your own:
I wish we could:

_____

_____

_____

_____

6. Intimacy and Sexuality

In any decade of marriage, the area of greatest struggle and greatest joy involves the gentle blend of intimacy and sexuality. The well-known writer Rollo May said, "Sex is the source of man's most intense pleasure and his most pervasive anxiety." Those of us who are living through our fifty-something years often have a clearer lens through which to view both the pleasure and the anxiety. We have an increasing need for marital and emotional intimacy as we grow older, and sexual expression is a vital part of that.

Yet we are intensely caught up in the myths surrounding our fifties decade that tell us we should not be as interested in sex today as we were when we were much younger. These myths also tell us we are now inexorably trapped in an era of declining sexual needs and physical attrition.

Writing in *Modern Maturity,* Arno Karlen said, "The myth is that age makes sexual pleasure fade and die. The truth is that middle and late life give us a second chance at sexual pleasure and harmony, often a better one than we had in youth. As we start speaking more honestly about sex in maturity, more people may seize that chance." Medical science has long confirmed that the sexual system is like the rest of our body; it will age but still function extremely well late in life. Dr. Howard Clinebell, in his classic book *The Intimate Marriage,* stated, "If couples revitalize their relationship during their middle years, there is no reason for sexual intimacy to decline. In fact, it can become deeper and richer because it includes the joys and heartaches, the accomplishments and disappointments, the storms and the peace of years of sharing each other's worlds."

One fifty-something friend described married sexuality in this decade as "either heating up, cooling down, or staying the same as always." He added that the major changes he enjoyed most were that he and his wife no longer had to worry that she would get pregnant—and now they could leave the bedroom door unlocked! While most of us can appreciate these advantages, we're also looking for deeper things. When intimacy is absent or deteriorates, indifference and isolation between husband

and wife can build walls of misunderstanding. Dr. Clinebell warns that "when sexual intimacy is lost, it is usually because of unresolved emotional conflicts within and between married partners."

Another factor may also contribute to a lack of sexuality in the fifty-something years. To treat high blood pressure some men and women may be taking medication that inhibits their sexual desire and performance. If this is so in your marriage, talk to your doctor. Sometimes the medication can be changed to another one that is less detrimental to sexual intimacy.

Finally, we revitalize ourselves and our marriages by taking time to enjoy life. Husbands and wives who have spent many years studiously devoting themselves to caring for family needs often discover in their fifty-something years that they have lost the capacity to just have fun. We are used to planning the fun while our children enjoy it. Now it's our turn to rediscover fun for ourselves. I say *rediscover* because it's not always easy for us to let go of our prim-and-proper fifty-something decorum and have fun again as we did when we were children. The older we get, the more rigid and inflexible we tend to become. We may have seen society frown on fifty-something people having fun in public (or even in private), so we tune our spirits to match our somber demeanor. No wonder the bumper sticker has to ask, "Are we having fun yet?"

Don't let your responsibilities rob you of the pleasure that's potentially yours. Rearrange your priorities, put your problems on hold, and give yourself permission to lighten up a little. *Have fun!* Then, when you see that bumper sticker again, you can joyfully answer *Yes!*

4

Women: Thriving through the Fifties

A woman should be able to be both independent and dependent, active and passive, relaxed and serious, practical and romantic, tender and tough-minded, thinking and feeling, dominant and submissive. So, obviously, should a man!

Pierre Mornell

ACROSS THE COUNTRY, there is a rising tide of fifty-something women who are coming alive with the options and opportunities before them. They are welcoming a positive transformation through renewal and redirection and making a mental and emotional shift from devotion to family to focus on self. For the first time in their lives, many of these women can honestly ask the question, "What do I really want to do with the rest of my life?"

Many of them want to experience the competition and challenge their husbands have talked about during the years of their vocational pursuit. Baking and cleaning are falling victim to salaries and promotions. Scores of fifty-something women are finding they have marketable gifts, talents, and abilities that can be used successfully in the workplace.

One fifty-something man recently described his newly working spouse as a "killer wife." When I asked for a definition, he replied that his once-passive homemaker wife had undergone some strange transformation since she entered the job market. She had become aggressive, competitive, and highly motivated to succeed at her newly chosen field. (I silently wondered what would happen if all the "killer wives" met each other on the playing field of corporate life!)

Recent studies support this perplexed husband's observation; they show that in women the need for achievement increases with age while the same need in men declines. Women also become more assertive with age while men tend to become more passive. Analysts of human nature could conclude that these role changes are a prelude to a new revolution between the sexes. Men may be threatened by women who are now in pursuit of a dream that once was exclusively male property. These trends can easily become divisive within fifty-something marriages as resentment builds when husbands desire to ease into the slow lane of life while their wives are accelerating in the fast lane.

It will take patience and understanding for husbands and wives to work through these unusual dynamics of change that could result in "ego invasions." The invasion has all the possibilities of robbing the other person (in this case it's usually the husband) of his identity. It takes a very secure husband to allow his wife to pursue her dream when he knows her success may become greater than his own.

Sometimes, however, the husband joins the woman in her success. That's what happened when Marie started a cheesecake-catering business just as her husband, Bruce, was retiring from his job with a grocery-store chain. For years, Marie's friends had told her she ought to "go into business" with the delicious cheesecakes she made. Finally, she did.

Because Marie's business got started while Bruce was still employed, he had little to do with it at first. But when he retired, he started helping by occasionally making deliveries. Next, because he was accustomed to working with wholesalers, he offered to order supplies for the cheesecakes from his former contacts in the grocery chain. When he placed his first order with these suppliers, who in many cases were longtime acquaintances, he made a point of meeting them in person so he could offer them samples of Marie's cheesecake. They, in turn, passed along recommendations to some of their other clients.

Before long, Marie's cheesecakes were enjoying a burst of sales, and both Marie and Bruce were enjoying being equal partners in the business. While Marie supervised the baking and recipe adaptations, Bruce handled the purchasing and marketing. They worked together to create new ideas for holiday tie-ins and other promotions.

It wasn't the retirement Bruce had planned, but he said, "I'm enjoying it, and I'm spending more time with Marie than I would be doing if I had the retirement I'd expected. Without this business I'd be spending most of my time with other retired men on the golf course or out on the lake in a fishing boat while Marie spent time working or being with her friends. This way we're spending time together—and doing something productive too."

Which Kind of Fifty-Something Woman Are You?

Not all fifty-something women suddenly turn into "killer wives." I believe fifty-something women in the

1990s can be divided into four basic groups. The first group contains the *nurturers,* those women who have adjusted to the middle years by accepting their roles as wives, mothers, and grandmothers. Their energies in part are still focused on meeting the needs of their children, husbands, and home. Outside activities may include volunteer work and some part-time employment, but their identities are largely tied to the vocation of their husband, the careers of their older children, and the care and nurturing of grandchildren.

A second group is made up of *discoverers,* those who are deeply involved in reworking the structure of their lives by pursuing a career or vocation on a full-time basis. This is the group that contains the killer wives, women who were once a quieter part of the nurturers group but are now intent on redirecting their lives in new areas. Further education is often a mandate for them as they add to the swelling ranks of mid-lifers on college campuses around the country.

The third group is composed of *achievers,* women who have worked diligently at a career for most of their lives while also raising a family. Now, with their children grown and living on their own, these women often work harder than ever at achieving success in their chosen fields. They pull out all the stops and run at top speed in their fifties.

The fourth group, called *displaced homemakers* in many reentry programs across the country, contains a growing number of fifty-something women who are forced into the job market due to a divorce or the illness or death of a spouse. Many in this group have worked little or not at all in the business world. They face retraining, education, interviewing, and low starting salaries as obstacles to their future in the workplace.

In all the research and surveys conducted in preparation for this book, I discovered that the nurturers seem to comprise the smallest portion of fifty-something women today while the largest group appears to be the discoverers. These must have been the women feminist writer Gloria Steinem was describing when she spoke at a recent symposium for older women. "This age group is the red-hot center of the revolution," she said. "The increased longevity and health is making this age group over fifty the critical mass of the changes to come." She summed up this group as being at the center of adventure and learning.

Losing and Winning

Many successful women who are traveling through their fifties are well aware that the options, opportunities, and successes they are now winning were preceded by losses. For many women, the biggest loss was that of their maternal role. The sense of being needed for things as simple as sewing on a button to things as important as discussing dating struggles usually keeps the mother at the center of her family's adventures. From the mundane to the intricate, a mother's image and success are often closely linked to her children. She wears the hats of coach, quarterback, manager, cheerleader, cleanup crew, nurse, cook, and confidante.

One fifty-something woman said, "I wish I had realized how important I was during these years. I was the center of the family. Instead, I often felt torn in pieces by all the different needs. Now that my children are gone I realize how lucky I was."

As this woman said, these daily nurturing and caring duties cease when the last child leaves home. This loss leaves many mothers displaced and "unemployed" as primary caregivers. When they no longer feel needed and when no new roles quickly appear to replace the ones that were lost, some mothers fall into times of depression and fear. Their identities disappear and the primary question becomes, *Who am I now?*

For many women, this displacement means losing the same things their husbands lose when a job or career ends: *belonging, meaning,* and *identity.*

Loss in any area of life can only be resolved by acceptance and rebuilding. Both processes take time. When affirmation is no longer received from meeting the needs of her children, the wife's natural inclination is often to seek it from her husband. This can start with the question, "Do you think we are still an attractive couple?" and proceed to "Do you think I am still attractive?" All the while the underlying question is really, "Am I still important to anyone in this house, and will you still love me when I don't look as good as I once did?"

This is the time a wife needs attentiveness and love more than ever. If it does not come from her husband, she may go seeking not only a new career but also a person who will give her a feeling of affirmation and acceptance. The important questions in life cannot remain unanswered.

You can help yourself overcome feelings of displacement by remembering that when your children leave home you do lose something, but it's not your children. Instead it's your position in the center of their lives.

More importantly, you also gain many new things in these changing roles. In most cases when children become separate entities, their relationships with their parents get better. For example, mother-daughter relationships usually reach a new level of growth when each woman's autonomy is not threatened and each is capable of reciprocation, care, and assistance. Many other gains will become evident with the passing of time.

In any turning point you will face new challenges with both fears and barriers.

Overcoming Fears and Barriers

In one of our workshops I recently listened to the stories of some fifty-something women who were trying to find employment. Their rejections went from "You're underqualified" to "You're overqualified" to "Leave your application; we'll call you if something comes up." Many of those who passed initial interviews discovered that starting salaries were barely above minimum wage. It is hard to be charged with optimism when you're faced with these realities. Those involved in retraining and reentry often wonder if the welfare line is not more amicable.

But most fifty-something women know that challenges and opportunities are almost always surrounded by barriers and fears. Some of the fears faced by women during this decade of decision are revealed by recent statistics:

- About 95 percent of women who are widowed after age fifty-five will never remarry.
- Half of all suicides of women happen after age forty-five.

- After the year 2000, 47 percent of the work force will be female.
- The average caregiver is a woman in her fifties.
- Older women are joining the ranks of the poverty-stricken faster than any other group in this country. The poverty rate for women over sixty-five is almost twice the rate for men of the same ages according to the U.S. Census.
- Women tend to outlive men. As a result, there are far more older women than men.
- Divorces among fifty-something couples are increasing more rapidly than in any other age group.
- Lack of finances and declining health are the two greatest fears among all fifty-something women we surveyed. Living the remainder of life alone is the third fear.

This list is not intended to send you running for the exit from life but to help you identify your fears and barriers so you can work to overcome them. Remember that growth is always dangerous—and glorious. I watch many people cave in to the obvious and allow their dreams and growth to be captured by their fears.

But remember, you have a choice: *You will either live your fears or live your dreams.*

If your barrier is a lack of marketable skills, one of the best sources of retraining is your local community college, most of which specialize in helping students discover their gifts, talents, and interests. Professionals there can also show you how to receive the best training possible for the job or career you desire, and they follow through by teaching you how to prepare a résumé and handle job interviews. Best of all, it doesn't cost very much. Besides community colleges, most cities have other schools and agencies with similar programs.

Many agencies that place workers in various jobs on a temporary basis offer some training in basic office skills, or they can refer you to local schools or colleges where you can get training for jobs that are in demand in your area. Although "temps" earn less money than those in equivalent permanent jobs, this is a good way to ease yourself into the job market, and it helps you decide what type of work will be most rewarding for you.

No matter how they go about it, fifty-something women who are facing the potentially ego-damaging process of entering or reentering the job market need support systems that can instill affirmation and self-worth in large doses. Generally, the married fifty-something woman has a built-in support group; her husband and family can cheer and encourage her through a sea of setbacks and rejections. In contrast, the single-again fifty-something woman is often left alone to face the discouragements of rebuilding. When support is lacking, alienation and a lack of self-confidence can take over and lead to a massive overdose of depression. That's why reentry workshops and similar programs for women are so valuable.

It's not always easy, but we can all learn to ride smoothly over things that go bump during the fifty-something years.

Riding Smoothly Over Things That Go Bump

Today's fifty-something woman faces both inner and outer changes in her life. Two examples of the turning points in the fifty-something years that can cause a bump in a woman's life are physical aging and changes in lifestyle. Let's take a closer look at each.

Physical Aging

In her book *Celebrating Fifty* Karen Blaker says, "Turning fifty is a second coming of age because it involves many of the same impulses and emotions that were present in our youth." Most of us can still remember those impulses and emotions. For example, always looking great and being popular were youthful obsessions. Your fifty-something mirror may still be sending you the same messages.

The struggle of being fifty-something is to attempt to still look great with a body that seems to thwart every honest effort you invest in it. Laugh lines and crow's-feet expand overnight into canyons with crisscrossing trails. Muscles once firm now take on the movements of your best Jell-o salad.

"Historically, women have suffered the double-edged sword of aging," said Shirley A. Waskel in her book *Midlife Issues and the Workplace of the '90s.* "Our culture highly esteems and respects attractiveness and beauty in women. As women in their middle years continue to experience changes in appearance and energy levels, they can become less than acceptable to spouses and others in society."

Physical aging is seldom laughed at or joked about by fifty-something women—including my wife, who has this to say about the things that go *bump* in her life:

Fifty-something for me is a place of frightful feelings, physical changes, and myriad wonders. I feel that I am no longer a part of the "beautiful people," the "leaders" of society, the "attractive" ones. I have now passed that stage, and others see me as someone who needs to slow down, get ready for some kind of retirement, and definitely get out of their way. I am now supposed to follow younger people. I don't like feeling that I'm the oldest person in various situations. It is a constant reminder of my aging.

My eyes seem to need examining about every three days; I have too many pairs of eyeglasses that keep disappearing. I have an awesome collection of brown spots on my hands. Extra weight is easy to put on and hard to take off even though I eat less than I ever did.

My skin is not what it used to be, and exercise and creams don't seem to make a dent. Menopause (that great period of mystery and dread) appears to have affixed itself to my life as a permanent nemesis. It attacks my femininity and gives me feelings of inadequacy and despair. My childbearing years are past, and even though I no longer desire pregnancy, I'm sometimes sensitive about my lack of choice. My mood swings wage war with my hot flashes. (I'd like to know why they call them *flashes* when they last for five and ten minutes!) And I'm usually pooped every day by three o'clock in the afternoon.

I spend too much time thinking about what I did right or wrong in raising my children. I am still working on shifting from thinking of them as "my children" to "married adults."

I know what is behind me, but I still wonder about what is ahead. Will there be time left to still do all the things I enjoy?

Yet the positives of being fifty-something outweigh the negatives: the wonder of grandchildren. It is very special to me to just enjoy them, play with them, and giggle with them. I relish the freedom to love and enjoy them unconditionally without the financial burdens a parent has.

I have a more accurate sense of time now and a better understanding of what's important to spend my time on. I'm less hurried and I savor the present without thinking so much about the future.

The fifties decade has been a time when I have started pleasing myself and letting go of things that are no longer necessary. I'm finally realizing I can trust myself and my judgments. I do many things now just for the mere pleasure of doing them, replacing some of the obligations I felt I once had to do.

For both of us as husband and wife it's more of an "us" time than a "them" time when the children were at home. It is a time of peace and love and contentment.

Carol at fifty-something

There are some ways to compensate for the natural effects of aging that Carol mentions. One was mentioned by Eda LeShan in her book *Oh, to Be 50 Again!* She says she finds it helpful to

reflect on which activities are likely to make me forget about the fact that I am getting older and which activities remind me most often . . . of the aging process. When I'm riding on a carousel, I feel eight years old; when I'm being fitted for special inserts for my shoes in order to minimize the pain from arthritic spurs, I feel old. . . . When I'm hugging (or being hugged by) Larry, I am never more than thirty-two, but when I am doing something for somebody else that I don't want to do and feel exploited, I am the oldest living woman left in the world.[1]

Another method used by LeShan is to "very quickly, without any time to think, write down a series of memories—the first ten that come into my mind." Then she analyzes those memories for "threads of importance" in her current life. The memory of a "nighttime high-school trip," for instance, reminds her of "my idea of what education ought to be like . . . a reminder that I learn best and most by doing and always have."[2]

Still another way to overcome the natural effects of aging—like the weight gain Carol mentions—is to slow down some of these changes by accepting the responsibility to take care of your body.

The Challenge to Stay Healthy. We are responsible for ourselves, including our physical health, and we have greater influence over our health than we often realize. Physical decline and bodily malfunctions cannot be denied, but we must try to keep them from commanding our entire attention to the point of becoming obsessive and controlling. And we certainly don't want other people to be obsessive and controlling about our age either!

In her book *Oh, to Be 50 Again!* Eda LeShan wrote, "During the winter when I was fifty-nine years old, I was shoveling the snow in my driveway. A neighbor rushed out of her house and ran over to me. 'You're too old for that, it's dangerous!' she said. It was a loving and protective impulse on her part, but I went into the house to look at myself in the mirror, trying to see what she saw. It was a shock—for the first time I was really aware of new wrinkles and graying hair."[3]

Love, happiness, and a large daily dose of optimism can powerfully impact our mental and physical health, even when "new wrinkles and graying hair" begin to appear in our mirrors. Authors Nolen and Pratt suggest that "those of us in mid-life need to organize our lives so as to experience more sheer pleasure. People are about as healthy as they make up their minds to be." Positive self-management is one of the most powerful tools we have to overcome negative experiences.

In their fifty-something journey, along with the physical "bump" of aging, women may have to contend with increased stress levels, loss of family and friends through death, fear of their own death, menopausal changes, a slump in physical fitness, and the need to care for older parents or relatives. All of these stressors can lead fifty-something women down their own pathway to depression. Although the causes for depression may be different in women than in men (see Chapter 5) the end result is the same: Depressed people are the walking dead in the land of the living.

It takes a strong program of positive change and rigid discipline to move out of depression. Often professional help can be very beneficial in achieving this return to healthy living.

A second turning point in the fifty-something years is a change in lifestyle.

Surviving a Change in Lifestyle

A frequent bump in the lives of many fifty-something women is a dramatic change in lifestyle due to their spouse's (or their own) job loss or career change. I have worked with many men who, during this difficult transition, have said they were afraid to tell their wives the truth about their situation. Wives who have said for years, "I don't know what I would do if you lost your job or if anything happened to you," have issued a warning against the sharing of harsh realities. If the husband is already traumatized by his loss and knows his wife will be similarly affected, he will often hide the truth as long as possible. (We'll take a closer look at the dynamics of a lost job or career in Chapter 8.)

When a husband or wife loses something vital to his or her survival and identity, that spouse desperately needs the other mate to be an understanding buffer and cheerleader. The quality of a married relationship is always tested in such times of struggle. When dramatic lifestyle changes come crashing down on them, some wives may fall apart and contribute little hope and healing to the marriage. Others will rise to new heights and become towers of strength and affirmation, offering support and understanding to their husbands in the time of crisis.

I recommend that women take a moment to call a time-out during their fifty-something years to establish their own individual plan and goals.

Calling a Time-Out to Establish a Plan
and Set Goals

Discoverers and achievers may find it easier than nurturers or displaced homemakers to survive these bumps as well as others that are more devastating, like divorce or the death of a spouse. This may happen because the nurturers or displaced homemakers have never explored the possibility of role changes and ways to take care of themselves financially. Economic self-sufficiency was seldom taught during the childhood years of today's fifty-something generation of women.

It *is* difficult to survive this kind of loss. But thousands of women have been through this experience and have come "out of the fire" with new confidence and the belief that they're now strong enough to face anything life throws their way.

Nancy was one of those women. When her husband of twenty-four years suddenly announced that he "needed time alone," she stood by in shock as he moved his things out of the house and into an apartment on the other side of the city. At first she was too hurt to even try to comfort her two teenage daughters, who were crushed by their father's departure.

"Gradually I realized that there was no one around to wave a wand or say the magic words to make things better. If I was going to survive this, it was up to *me*," she said.

She approached a local women's group about its scholarship fund when she saw a notice in the city's newspaper about the group's outreach to displaced homemakers. She won the scholarship and attended classes at a technical school to get training in graphic arts and typesetting.

Soon Nancy found a rewarding job with a local printing firm, where she was praised not only for her new skills but also for her dependability and her ability to work with customers—characteristics of maturity.

Regardless of which category she's in, the fifty-something woman needs to establish some goals and a plan as she considers her future. Persons who have a working plan will always feel more secure than those who feel things will go on the same way forever. Most goals fall into three categories: short-term, intermediate-term, and long-term. You need to have a sprinkling of all three in your planning. If all your goals are long-term, the danger is you will never start on them. If all your goals are short-term, you will accomplish them too easily and lack challenge. Goals need to be shared with others so you are held accountable. When you achieve a goal, celebrate your success with others who have given you their affirmation and support.

Take time in the next week to consider the following list as ideas for your goals. This exercise will guide you in developing relational, personal, vocational, spiritual, financial, educational, family, health, lifestyle, and contingency goals.

Developing Goals

1. Relational goals

Who do I need in my life as part of an ongoing support system that will be in place no matter what might happen to me?

_____

_____

Are my friendships:

_____ deep or

_____ shallow?

Is it time to build some new friends into my life?

_____ yes   _____ no

Do some of my friends have a toxic effect on me so that I need to let them go? _____ yes   _____ no

If so, list them below:

_____

_____

_____

2. Personal goals

Complete the statements that follow to develop your personal goals for yourself.

Some personal accomplishments I would like to complete in my life are:

_____

_____

_____

Are these goals:

_____ mine or

_____ someone else's goals for me?

If I attain them, what will that mean in my life?

_____

How have my personal goals changed over the years?

_____

_____

_____

Is it time to reclaim any once-delayed goals?

_____ yes _____ no

3. Vocational goals

What do I want to do vocationally for some of the rest of my life?

_____

_____

Are these goals:
_____ someone else's or
_____ are they mine?

What is the price tag on my vocational goals? (How long will they take and what will I really have when I get there?)

_____

_____

Do I have all the formal education I need to pursue a new vocation?

_____ yes _____ no

Will further education mean a better income for me?
_____ yes _____ no

Will short-term sacrifices be worth long-term gains?
_____ yes
_____ no

Are my goals in this area unrealistic because the vocation is becoming obsolete? _____ yes _____ no

What will the monetary gain be?

_____

4. Spiritual goals

What do I want to attain in my spiritual growth?

_____

How important is the spiritual dimension in my life?
_____ very important
_____ one of my considerations
_____ not so important

I can count on the following spiritual friends to support me in this area:

_____

_____

Am I in the right church for me? _____ yes _____ no

What do I want to give to others spiritually?

_____

_____

5. Financial goals

What kind of shape am I in financially?

_____ I (or we) have the necessary savings and debt-free position to retire at sixty-five if I (or we) want to.

_____ I (or we) will probably have to continue working after age sixty-five.

What would it take to get to where I need to be?

_____

_____

What do I need to change about the way I handle money?

_____

_____

If difficult times come financially, what will my game plan be to handle them?

_____

_____

6. Family goals

What are our greatest assets as a family?

_____

_____

What are our liabilities?

_____

_____

Are some of our family members still living without forgiveness from others in the family?

_____ yes   _____ no

How can we become the kind of family I would like to be a part of?

_____

_____

_____

_____

7. Health goals

What kind of shape am I in physically?

_____ good

_____ fair

_____ poor

What kind of shape would I *like* to be in physically?

_____

What kind of physical disciplines do I need to develop?

_____

_____

When was the last time I had a physical checkup from my family doctor?

_____

8. Contingency goals

How many of my goals do I have complete control over? _____

How many of my goals are under someone else's control? _____

How often do I surrender leadership of my goals to others? _____

_____ very often

_____ sometimes

_____ infrequently

_____ never.

Do I surrender my goals so I will not have to be accountable for any failures? _____ yes _____ no

What goals do I need to maintain ownership of?

_____

_____

_____

The eight goals listed here are not for fifty-something women alone. They can be equally used by husbands, other family members, and friends.

The most positive thing a goal does is keep us focused. We all tend to suffer from scattered attention. Staying in focus is a form of discipline that gives direction to our lives. It helps us to live the adventure.

Living the Adventure

Your decade of being a fifty-something woman will be what you make it. If you decide you need to add a little extra zest to this stage of your life, you might get some ideas from Madin Stair of Louisville, Kentucky. When she was eighty-five years old, she wrote the following words:

If I had my life to live over, I'd care to make more mistakes next time. I would limber up. I would be sillier than I have been this trip. I would take fewer things seriously. I would take more chances. I would climb more mountains and swim more rivers. I would perhaps have more actual troubles, but I'd have fewer imaginary ones.

You see, I'm one of those people who lives sensibly and sanely, hour after hour, day after day. Oh, I've had my moments, and if I had to do it over again, I'd have more of them. In fact, I'd try to have nothing else. Just moments, one after another, instead of living so many years ahead of each day.

I've been one of those persons who never goes anywhere without a thermometer, a hot water bottle, a raincoat, and a parachute. If I had to do it again, I would travel lighter than I have. If I had my life to live over, I would start barefoot earlier in the spring and stay that way later in the fall. I would go to more dances. I would ride more merry-go-rounds. I would pick more daisies.

Fifty-something is a long way from being eighty-five! In all likelihood you have a lot of years left to exercise new freedoms and throw away old cautions.

5

Becoming One's Own Man: Booming in the Fifties

When a sleeping man wakes up, he catches fire with the spirit of new possibilities for his life.
Merle Fossom

SOME YEARS AGO Daniel Levinson, the noted researcher and writer about men, coined the term *BOOM*, for Becoming One's Own Man. Levinson's premise was that this "becoming" process slipped into gear rather quietly and effortlessly as a man moved from one decade to another. Along the way, Levinson said, each man passed through certain definitive passageways that culminated eventually in a higher form of male adulthood.

The goal of becoming one's own man may be more on target today than it was twenty years ago, but the journey to get there is definitely rockier and filled with greater obstacles than ever before. The rite of easy passage has been replaced by a wrestling match with the dragons of destruction, like the pressures of being a good provider and husband in today's world where the women's expectations are so high and the economy is so weak. In fact, the fifty-something man of the 1990s bears little resemblance to his predecessors from earlier decades.

The decade of the nineties may go down in history as the era of the men's movement. Many things are changing as men are taking a closer look at who they really are and what their role is in family, vocation, and life. Author Robert Bly ignited the fuse in his book *Iron John* when he advocated a return to a primal type of man who could portray a sense of ruggedness, myth, and story.

Sam Keen added another perspective with *Fire in the Belly*; he suggested that men seek a new personal ideal of strength, potency, and manhood along with the ability to be both tough and tender.

The movie *City Slickers* graphically brought the struggle into view. I think every man in the theater the night I attended wanted to be Billy Crystal for two weeks— or perhaps the rest of his life! We watched as he left his high-rise, New York executive job to spend two weeks as a ranch hand. He roped cows, rode in a roundup, helped deliver a baby calf, and felt the roughness of the earth beneath him as he slept under the stars. Whereas in the corporate world he couldn't see the result of the endless meetings and mindless paperwork, he now felt as if he was doing something real, something tangible.

Unfortunately, like Billy Crystal in his office job, most of us today don't see the end product of our efforts. We can't say, "I made that chair." But on the ranch Billy Crystal could say, "I delivered that calf. I brought life into the world. I know who I am. I have a purpose."

In completing this fifties portion of the passage toward becoming your own man, remember what some insightful person once said: "There are three kinds of people in life: Those who watch things happen, those who make things happen, and those who don't know what's happening." Which one are you? The fifty-something man who falls into the second category will be more in control of his life and destiny than the one who is a spectator or the one who is lost in the fog.

Making things happen requires that we search for meaning in the midst of unplanned-for problems instead of racing by them in order to escape their pain.

Searching for Meaning in Unplanned-For Events

Unplanned-for changes can explode upon us, and we must find a way to fit them into our lives. This phenomenon is not unique to the fifties decade, of course; we have to deal with unexpected events throughout our lives. Realizing how often we've done so in the past gives us confidence that we can continue doing it in the future.

Because men are by nature more didactic than women, our search for meaning in the things that happen to us is often short-circuited. This also occurs because men are typically less process-oriented; we want to "fix" things that go wrong rather than explore the meanings behind them. In this way a man might never come to see that losing a job, a career, or a lifestyle could mean there is a better one for him in the next chapter of life.

Instead of rushing to "fix" changes that occur unexpectedly, take a time-out for a closer look and ask yourself these three questions, which always need to be asked at any change point:

- What does this change mean?
- What does this change mean to me?
- What does this change mean to those around me?

Answering these questions helps you search for the meaning in the event, itself, rather than the meaning of the event for those involved. For example:

- What does this change mean? *It may mean God is interrupting my life and plans.*
- What does this change mean to me? *It may mean that unused gifts, talents, and abilities in my life may be challenged for the first time.*
- What does this change mean to those around me? *Their lives may be forever different because of the changes I make.*

Abraham Lincoln is a vivid example of someone who found meaning in the events that happened to him. He lost some elections during his political career, but those losses became stepping-stones to his ultimate victory when he became president of the United States. In an 1858 election, Lincoln ran as the underdog in a race against Stephen A. Douglas for a U.S. Senate seat—and Lincoln lost. But he found meaning in the campaign, itself, not just its outcome, and he used that insight to further his political aspirations.

Douglas, the incumbent, was well known, and Lincoln realized that merely by being on the same debate platform with Douglas he would share in the spotlight that perpetuated the renowned senator's fame. It was during this unsuccessful campaign and its seven debates that Lincoln began to make a name for himself as an inspiring public speaker. This led to his addressing a political rally in New York in February 1860. By May of that year, he was popular enough to be nominated as a candidate for the presidency.

Starting Again When Dreams Are Shattered

If a man looks for meaning in the unexpected events that happen to him, he also knows the importance of looking inward. This is never more true than when a man begins the journey back from a midlife loss; restoration always starts with inner rebuilding. The old African proverb says it well: "If there's no enemy within, there's no enemy outside that can do us any harm."

Still, the challenge of rebuilding your inner self can at first seem overwhelming. As one writer noted, "In the long run, this awakening process can bring people deeper joy and meaning in their lives, but the beginning can be painful and difficult."[1]

When a man's dreams are shattered, his identity may also lie in ruin. Restoration and reconstruction from that point can be a grueling process that puts entire family systems under siege. I continually watch families fall apart under this kind of pressure when fathers and husbands, once thought to be powerful and capable of solving any problem, become immobilized, fearful, and haunted by the thought that they may never work or be productive again. Entangled in their circumstances and blinded by their fears, they often become their own worst enemy.

This was the case for a man named Chris, who in his mid-fifties was forced into early retirement due to increasingly frequent asthma attacks. The last one had come in the middle of a high-level business meeting two thousand miles from home and had required emergency medical treatment. Chris had been taken from the meeting site in an ambulance.

The next blow was an insurance company's refusal to

sell him a life-insurance policy. Both embarrassed and frightened by what was happening to him, Chris accepted his boss's suggestion that he take the company's generous early-retirement package and get out of the corporate rat race.

The rising-star corporate CPA who had always worn custom-made suits and gold cufflinks suddenly found himself wandering aimlessly around an empty house in his bathrobe while his wife was at work. Although he belonged to a health club and enjoyed playing golf, his recent asthma attacks had caused him to avoid those places. Alone at home, he pondered his future and grew increasingly depressed, sure that his next attack would be his last gasp.

He even began refusing to go out with his wife in the evenings when they were invited to friends' homes or for other social occasions, fearful that another attack would either cripple or embarrass him—or both. Besides, he seemed to have so little to contribute to the conversation. As he grew more introverted, his feelings of worthlessness grew; his wife became more frustrated with his "dropping out of life," and their marriage suffered.

Emotionally and economically, no age-group decade has been more impacted by situations like Chris's than those in their fifties. It is little wonder that depression is the most frequently treated mental illness among fifties men or that men between age forty-five and fifty-five commit two-thirds of all male suicides. Job-seeking organizations and related support groups are filled with fifty-something members—most often men—in cities large and small across America. For many of these men, these organizations offer not only a sympathetic ear but also a positive way out of their misery.

The turning point for Chris came when a friend asked him to help with an assignment from SCORE, the Service Corps of Retired Executives.

"Adam had volunteered to advise a young couple as they got a small business started up, and he just called to ask a question after the best arrangement for taxes," Chris said. "In their case it was a complicated issue and I had to do a little research before I was sure I had the answer. Then Adam wasn't sure he could accurately relay all the details I gave him, so he asked if I would mind doing a conference call with him and the young couple. I didn't even hesitate. I knew I wouldn't have to worry about making a scene if an attack came on. I was still at home in my bathrobe—I could just excuse myself and hang up! So I agreed—and when the call was over, I felt like my second chance at life had begun."

Now actively involved in SCORE, Chris is still plagued by occasional asthma attacks. "And the attacks still scare me—but they don't *embarrass* me so much anymore, and I'm able to come back from an attack and throw back my shoulders and go on with my life. Maybe it's because as an executive with a big paycheck I felt I wasn't supposed to have any weaknesses—and I certainly wasn't supposed to make scenes. But now, as a volunteer, I feel more human, and all human beings have weaknesses. Asthma just happens to be mine."

Chris had a strong support system, a positive belief in his gifts, talents, and abilities, and a solid trust that God was in charge. He also kept a journal as one way to explore his inner feelings. Each of these factors helped him to search for meaning in this unplanned-for event.

His fifty-something reality was ill health, one of the

common setbacks of these years. Let's look at some other realities that pose challenges for men in their fifties.

Wrestling with the Realities

We live in a culture that specializes in answers. When solutions are not forthcoming, we become impatient and distracted because grappling with issues long-term is not our forte. Unfortunately, many of the ongoing issues for fifty-something men do not have easy answers. They will remain unsolved but wrestled with in the dark hours of the night as well as in the bright light of day.

Here are five of the more acknowledged realities I have listened to in the past few years.

"I wish I had better friends like my wife has."

Men tend to have many *acquaintances* while women have more *friends*. This often occurs because men are unwilling to invest the energy it takes to establish meaningful friendships. Men can't just *be* with one another; they have to *do* something. Part of the problem for fifty-something men, in particular, is that they did not have the time to establish meaningful friendships with other men when they were so busy earning a living, often traveling throughout their region or the country three or four days a week. Now they may have more time to spend with friends—but they have none! I meet very few men who say they have two or three friends in their lives who would fall into the category of "intimate."

It may be more difficult to seek the friends you need as you grow older, but it is never too late if you are willing to invest your time and yourself in nurturing a relationship. I have sometimes mentioned the golf course as a negative dead end. Yet joining a men's golfing association at the local country club or public golf course can be a good way to make new friends. And most churches are looking for a man's input on many committees, particularly finance. Working together with other men is an excellent way to expand friendships.

"I've had enough hassles all my life with my work. I don't want any more."

Fifty-something men want to live as hassle-free as possible. Some say, "I've earned the right." Many men even reject the household hassles of fixing things, choosing to hire the work to be done by others. Suddenly, projects large or small can seem overwhelming.

The freedom of living more simply is a goal of these fifty-something men. In most cases, this is an admirable goal. If you're financially comfortable, there's nothing wrong with paying someone else to handle household hassles such as repairing broken toasters or changing the oil in your car or any job that involves heavy lifting. (It's worth saving your back from the extra strain and the possible plague of a chronic bad back.)

"I wish I had more energy."

A decline in physical energy is a reality for those living through the fifty-something decade, even if we don't have a physical illness like asthma, heart disease, or high blood pressure. Those who say it isn't true are lying to themselves. I know, because I have tried to play the denial game from time to time. I still run a few miles a day, and I attempt to play a mean game of racquetball, but I have learned that I just don't rebound as quickly as I once did.

Now the exercise has become more important to me than the final score; after all, there is nothing I need to prove anymore by winning. Catching a nap here and there has also become a new item on my agenda. (The secret is to avoid being caught!)

Adjustment is probably the key to surviving the loss of energy. I try to accept the fact that my energy level may decline as I age. But I remember that my body's need for exercise doesn't end as my energy level drops. Regular exercise—walking, swimming, playing a sport, or finding some other activity that gives my body a workout—still energizes me and helps keep me fit.

"I am in a dead-end job."

There was a time when you could leave any job almost at any age and find another one. With available jobs now vastly outnumbered by those applying for them and the economy flirting with recession or depression, this is no longer true. Blunted ambitions are staring hard realities in the face today. In this harsh economic climate many men in dead-end careers are happy to still be working, but they're miserable with what they're doing—and few things are more miserable than a job with no challenge.

Fortunately, there are still challenges in life outside of the workplace. I suggest that men find something to enjoy during their leisure hours that will add meaning to their life: Join a literacy group and teach someone to read, solicit broken bicycles from your church or neighborhood and repair them for needy children, or help build a house with a volunteer-builders program. Nurture an interest until it becomes a pleasurable hobby. Plant a garden. There are dozens of opportunities for similar diversions; find something to challenge yourself, then go after it!

"I missed all the road signs. My life today would have been vastly different if only . . . !"

We all spend too much time looking back over our shoulders, wishing *if only.* . . . I have done it and you have too. I once had the opportunity to buy some beachfront property with a friend on the Gulf of Mexico in Florida. The little amount of money I needed to join this real estate venture was small—but far more than I had in my bank account. I passed, and my friend bought the property without my financial assistance. Today, a resort hotel sits on the property. Guess who wouldn't be working so hard now if he had somehow bought into this piece of sparkling sand? It all adds up to nothing more than a big dose of regret and guilt.

I have never spent a lot of time looking back at the other losses in my own life. I am the kind of optimist who sees the sun going down in the West and rising in the East at the same minute. Somehow God has given me the ability to focus on the present and future with little time invested in past regrets. However I do have a mental memory file of a few other "wishes past":

- I wish I had learned the principle of "family first" on the first day of our marriage.
- I wish I would have learned the principle of sound financial planning on the second day of my marriage.
- I wish I had gotten all the formal education I would need by age thirty.
- I wish our family could have lived in the same city

for twenty-five years. (We moved many, many times.)

- I wish I had an answer to the question, "Where is home for you?"
- I wish I had not left the spiritual growth of my family up to the church.
- I wish we had not tried to mix family vacations with my seminar and ministry events for so many years.

All any of us can do is try to accurately read the present road signs and make wise decisions based upon that reading. Then, as someone said, "Forget the past; there's no future in it." A revised reading might say, "Learn from the past or you will have no future."

These are the hard realities of the fifty-something man, but there are also common joys in this passage of life.

The Joys of Becoming One's Own Man at Fifty-Something

Even if becoming one's own man is an experience relegated to later life, at least four profound joys are connected with it.

Giving and Receiving

An emerging development in the fifty-something years is a new kind of idealistic concern about younger people called "generativity." In broad form, it means having an older generation care more deeply about a younger one. It is a form of coaching that goes beyond the field of sports and into the everyday situations of life. The world needs a strong rebirth of this form of caring in fifty-something men. The recent census said there were more than sixteen million children living in the United States today without the influence of a father figure in their lives. That's an army deeply in need of generativity, mentoring, and guidance. Fifty-something is an opportune time for us to give something back to those climbing the mountain behind us.

"Leaving a legacy" is often described in terms of an estate, finances, or trust. But the inheritance of worldly possessions is a tiny fraction of what anyone has to pass along to others in this life. The fifties decade is a time to think about the legacy you will leave behind. Honor, courage, love, and values are legacies that are not designated in wills and trusts. If they are not passed on, they will die with the bearer. They can only be instilled by example and received with respect.

A river of change is flowing through maledom today. It is flooding both young and old with external forces they have no control over and propelling them uncontrollably toward its rapids where too often our sole concern is to keep from drowning. When life loses some of its predictability, we tend to grab for instant answers. Instead, what we really need is to totally reexamine the situation, in this case reassessing the male role in society. Fifty-something men might well become the catalyst for this latent phenomenon. We have lived long enough to know what hasn't worked and we have enough time left to model new ideas that can impact both the young and the old.

Taking Responsibility and Celebrating Recovery

Becoming one's own man at fifty-something may involve not only giving but taking—but not the kind of taking that you might expect. I'm talking about taking responsibility for past mistakes in living. Joining one of the many recovery programs available today is one positive way to do that. In these groups, long years of life-robbing addictions are finally being dealt with by many men in their fifties. I've noticed a sadness in men who have been heavy drinkers or have had uncontrollable tempers that have ruined so many years of their lives and the lives of those around them. The common question is, "Why didn't I do something about this years ago?"

I have also observed a new excitement about life in those who are celebrating their recovery process and looking forward to living a healthy existence in their remaining years. It is never too late for a new beginning!

It takes a great deal of courage and humility to ask for help from someone, even someone or some organization that is specifically trained or designed to provide assistance. Traditionally men have a more difficult time with this than women. Society has so typecast the male role that many men have become imprisoned within its rigid definitions. To break free means to cast the stereotypes aside and fearlessly build one's own personhood. It may be easier to strike out in this direction after fifty than earlier in life because now there is less worry about what others will think and more concern about self-definition. As a result, feeling good about yourself becomes more important than how others feel about you.

Enjoying a Deepening Spirituality

I listen to more and more fifty-something men talk about their desire to deepen their relationship with God and walk closer to Him. Some are reconnecting after years of being disconnected. Others are seeking connection for the first time. Many are nudged toward a spiritual confrontation by personal crises that have overpowered them. All have experienced a sense of powerlessness, and they recognize the need in their life for a higher power who can take control.

Recognition of that need and acting upon it can be called many things: a revelation, a step of faith, a conversion, a spiritual moment, an encounter with God, or other descriptive terms. Whatever it's called it must be followed by the journey of spiritual growth. Merle Fossom, author of *Catching Fire,* says, "For spiritual growth to happen, we have to let go of our attachment to rational, logical structure and risk the free-fall into nonrational experience. Facts are not always the same as truth. The leap of faith is a decision to rely sometimes on those things we cannot measure or prove objectively."

A deepening spirituality helps us make sense out of our earthly journey and gives us faith to accept the many things we don't understand. Spirituality puts us in closer touch with God and with ourselves. It helps us view the confusing events of life through a spiritual lens and know that some things will always defy human explanation.

Becoming one's own man spiritually means becoming a new man. Writing about "the new man of the '90s" in *Charisma,* former *Guideposts* editor Leonard LeSourd said, "The real 'new man' of the '90's is the same as the 'new man' St. Paul described 2,000 years ago." According to LeSourd he is the man who:

- Knows who he is in Christ.
- Knows why he is here on earth.
- Knows that God has a plan for his life.
- Is dependent on God.
- Is forgiving.
- Will take unpopular stands for what is right.

- Has a controlled aggressiveness.
- Is "others-centered."
- Feels free to fail or lose.
- Knows and seeks guidelines from Scripture.
- Sees his body as a temple of the Holy Spirit.
- Is a good role model.
- Is faithful and sacrificial as a husband.
- Is sensitive and caring as a father.
- Is a man of prayer.
- Has priorities in this order: God, family, work, others.[2]

Some fifty-something men reading this list are probably thinking, *Where were these standards when I was starting out on my manhood journey? I'm too far down the road to include these in my 'late life changes' agenda.*

Perhaps we should start a "Spiritual Manhood Recovery Program" and use the list as a sixteen-step program for growth. Many of these criteria have disappeared from the lives of those who have been church-connected all their lives. It is time to bring back scriptural directives to masculinity in any age. A growth-oriented man knows it is never too late for a new beginning. Here are some goals I've set to serve as ways to deepen my fifties faith:

1. I am working at spending more time each day with the Lord in meditation, prayer, reading Scripture, reading Christian literature, journaling, thinking, reflecting, and getting more in touch with my feelings.
2. I want to allow God to do things in my life that are bigger than I am.

3. I want to understand more deeply the sovereignty of God.
4. I want to spend less time "doing" and more time "being."
5. I want to explore the active work of the Holy Spirit in my life.
6. I want to be more transparent, open, and honest.
7. I want my faith to have "staying power."

Enjoying Family Relationships

Many of today's fifty-something men are still living out the Great Depression mentality of their parents. This mind-set was often played out in one of two ways. Because of their great losses, many victims of the depression later taught their children to buy or collect all the materialistic things they could because a similar experience could be around the next corner. I believe the roots of modern-day materialism grew out of this philosophy of "get what you can while you can." The other attitude had depression victims doing just the opposite: saving and hoarding every penny possible to prepare for the next big disaster. Either way, things—worldly goods or savings— became more important than people or experiences.

If this describes your past priorities, you may find yourself making a change as you begin the fifty-something journey toward becoming your own man.

For example, many men have said their families mean more to them at fifty-something than they did earlier in life. Perhaps the family that once meant confusion, chaos, and perpetual noise now means closeness, warmth, and a deeper bond. Many men want to create and experience some adventures with their older children and grandchildren that will go into the good-memories archives. Unfortunately, men at our age often vie for their children's time only to find that the children are now too busy moving their own lives along. Happily, though, young grandchildren can be much more accessible. Whatever time we spend making happy memories with any members of our family will be well worth our effort, even if it takes some skillful planning and accommodating.

Men in their fifties are often moved to invest more of their time, effort, and money in experiences and people—the memory-makers in life—instead of in things. Take a time-out to look at the following lists and consider your "investment" in each:

Things	**Experiences**
House	Family vacations
Automobile	Weekend outings
Furnishings	Foreign travel
Clothes	Mission trips
Adult toys	Seminars
Antiques	Educational growth experiences
Art	Self-improvement
Collectibles	Religious life
	Celebrations
	Retreats

These lists are neither good nor bad. They merely give you an opportunity to evaluate your priorities and think about how you might reframe them.

Because of all these realities of the fifty-something man, many male respondents to our survey felt their greatest need, in light of all the current ominous pressures on them, was to build hope into their daily lives. Without a strong infusion of hope each day, they said, they feared they would be buried in their fifties.

Adding Hope to Your Life

One way to fill your own life with hope is to plant it in others, as Chris, the asthmatic CPA, learned when he began volunteering to help new businesses get started. Try to do something good—even a small favor—for someone else every day. Whether it's just spending a few minutes listening—*really* listening—to a family member who wants to talk or anonymously dropping a quarter in someone's expired parking meter, as Alan Loy McGinnis says, "there is something therapeutic about doing another person a favor."[3]

Another way to instill hope in your life is through daily prayer and Bible reading. You might start with Romans 5:3–5:

We also glory in tribulations, knowing that tribulation produces perseverance; and perseverance, character; and character, hope. Now hope does not disappoint, because the love of God has been poured out in our hearts by the Holy Spirit who was given to us. (NKJV)

Use a concordance to find other verses that use the word *hope*. Memorize those that inspire you, then recite them to yourself often.

Many men also find hope and comfort in reflecting on happier times and remembering good experiences.

Becoming a Man of Value

For many men, fifty-something is a time of questioning, searching, and changing.

It is adding up wins and losses but realizing there is still prime time left to play the game.

It is looking at things differently and smiling to yourself more often, knowing you have learned things others still have to learn.

It is dreaming new dreams and knowing you can still catch the fire of new possibilities.

It is believing again the words of Albert Einstein: "Try not to become a man of success. Rather become a man of value."

6

Single Again at Fifty-Something

Becoming single again is not a death sentence. It is an opportunity to take full responsibility for your own life and growth.

Jim Smoke

NAVIGATING THE FIFTY-SOMETHING years with a spouse alongside is difficult enough. Taking the journey alone can be a perilous, defiant, and scary experience. But that is happening to growing numbers of men and women who, by death or divorce, are single again at fifty-something.

This increase is apparent in such places as churches' singles groups, where the fastest-growing age group is the forty- to sixty-year-old crowd. It is also obvious in my own experience. Almost half of the people in the divorce-recovery seminars I have held around the country have been married more than twenty-five years.

There are two main reasons for the increasing numbers of older singles in our country: First, our society as a whole is aging, and second, the number of divorces taking place today after twenty-five to forty years of marriage is increasing significantly.

The Battle for a New Beginning

For more than two decades I have listened to the fears, struggles, and celebrations of single-again people. I have watched them mourn over a life script that was never completed, and I have given my support as they wrote a new script and fought to live it out. Finally, I have cheered as they moved beyond their hurt to healing and hope.

Gene was one of those fighters. His wife of thirty years was killed in a car crash just as Gene was retiring from a long and successful military career. In the last four years of their marriage they had been planning to start a new adventure together when Gene retired. They had spent four thousand dollars on training to become travel agents and had just begun part-time work in a friend's agency when Clara died.

"We had always traveled a lot with the military, and we had enjoyed seeing the world," Gene recalled. "Clara and I thought we had a lot to offer travelers as far as experience and advice. And we also planned to take advantage of our part-time work and the discounts travel agents receive and do a lot of traveling ourselves, to places we hadn't been. It was a dream we had shared and nurtured to reality. And then that dream was destroyed in one split second on the freeway."

Devastated by Clara's sudden death, Gene quit his new job and withdrew into an empty shell of despair and grief. Within a single year he had left a meaningful career and lost his lifetime partner; it was almost too much to bear. By the time his adult children finally persuaded him to see a counselor he had lost twenty pounds and appeared gaunt and disheveled.

The counselor helped him join a support group of people in similar circumstances, and gradually Gene was able to see that there was a future for him beyond the pain he was feeling. Four months later, his friend called from the travel agency and asked if Gene would be willing to help out "just during the holiday crunch." Reluctantly, he agreed. Two years later, he's still there.

"I wish I could say I went back to work and everything was rosy again, but that didn't happen," he said later. "The pain was still there, and a lot of times when I arranged a trip to some exotic place I would remember that Clara and I had planned to go there. Then the grief would hit again like a sledgehammer. But over all, each day became a little easier, maybe because I was busy. Then some good things started happening. People I had helped started asking for me again when they called the agency. A few of them even called back later to say they had enjoyed the tour I had arranged for them or they loved the restaurant I had recommended to them. A couple of them even told me they had met people on their trip who had paid a lot more for their tickets than they had, so they were recommending me to their friends. It makes me feel productive and needed, and that has helped a lot."

The battle for a new beginning after what seems like a final ending often takes two to three years. There are no instant answers or miracle cures to help you go from sharing responsibilities to assuming responsibilities. If you began moving into your fifty-something decade expecting it to be the prime time in your life, the loss of a spouse by death or divorce hits you with a double whammy: not only the loss of your mate, but also the loss of your dreams. But there *is* life after divorce or the death of a spouse. It may be painful and it's certainly hard work to establish this new life, but millions of fifty-something people have met these challenges and successfully started over. You can too.

After dealing with the unexpectedness of your loss, the next greatest challenge will be to deal with your fears.

Naming Your Fears

Alone at fifty-something, the fears that come into our lives can immobilize us. Instead of choosing to move ahead and create our own plans, we can let our fears trap us in a state of constant paralysis.

We've already said that fears must be identified before they can be overcome. The following list contains some of the most frequently expressed fears I hear from single-again fifty-something people. Respond to each one as it relates to you.

Common Fears among Single-Again People at Fifty-Something

	Yes	No
1. The fear of living alone.	_____	_____
2. The fear of growing old alone.	_____	_____
3. The fear of never marrying again.	_____	_____
4. The fear of failing health with no one to care for me.	_____	_____
5. The fear of losing my job or career.	_____	_____
6. The fear of economic disaster.	_____	_____
7. The fear of losing old friends from my married years.	_____	_____

8. The fear of having to relocate geographically.   _____ _____

9. The fear of abusing my relationships.   _____ _____

10. The fear of not having a strong support system in my life.   _____ _____

11. The fear of having to change my lifestyle. _____ _____

12. The fear of having to reenter the work force after many years of not working.   _____ _____

13. The fear of how a death or divorce will impact my family.   _____ _____

14. The fear that life will no longer be worth living by myself.   _____ _____

15. The fear that I will not be able to handle the things I never had to handle.   _____ _____

16. The fear of failure.   _____ _____

All these fears can be very real if you find yourself single again at fifty-something, and you get little help from those who tell you, "Don't worry about that. You will be fine." These fears do not go away by themselves. To deal with them, you have to name them and build a plan to confront and resolve them. In this section, we'll look at ways to deal with the most common of the single-again fears.

The Fear of Living Alone

It may sound strange, but the fear of living alone can be resolved by *learning how to do it!* Begin by attacking your specific worries. If your greatest fear in living alone is that someone will break into your residence and rob, rape, or mug you, install the best security system you can find. If your fear is the silence of an empty house, fill your home with music and sound. If your fear is coming home to an empty house or apartment, get a pet who will be eager to see you at the end of the day. If your fear is not knowing how to care for your home, take classes in home maintenance at the local community college. If your fear is lack of human companionship, find a roommate you can share and enjoy your life with. I have worked with many people who have used these suggestions and discovered that their fear has dissolved.

The Fear of Growing Old Alone

Several fears on the list are linked to the fear of growing old alone. The very process of aging seems to increase the risk that we will be rejected by others, because many people simply do not seem to want to spend their time with older men and women.

The best way to have the support of friends later is to have their support *now*. By building a strong community of friends who love and care about you, you can be reassured that you will not be alone. (We'll discuss the subject of friends in more detail in Chapter 13.)

The Fear of Never Marrying Again

For many single-again people in their fifties the fear of never marrying again tops the list. In his book *Racing Toward 2001,* author Russ Chandler says, "Older single women, either divorced or widowed, are the fastest growing group in America. By 2001, half of the persons over 65 will be single, with women in this category outnumbering men by a 3 to 1 margin."

Those are ominous statistics for men or women desiring remarriage after a death or divorce in their fifties. But remember, you are not a statistic until you have lived out the prophecy! The key to any thoughts of remarriage is to become a vibrant, healthy, growing person within yourself. Healthy, happy people attract healthy, happy people. The statistics may be gloomy, but there is still room for tremendous hope and optimism. Many people do marry again in their fifties and, I might add, live happily ever after.

The Fear of Losing a Job or Career

People who are single *again* at fifty-something have already endured one loss through either divorce or the death of their spouse. As a result they may focus even more on their jobs or careers than do people who have spouses who share their lives. When anything changes that focal point, the fallout from it can impact other areas in the single person's life with a domino effect. For example, the fear of losing a job or career is almost always coupled with economic fears. And if those fears become realities, another fear, the fear of a changing lifestyle, may follow. (We'll discuss specifics of the fifty-something job loss in Chapter 8.)

If fear says *I might lose something,* trust says *I can find something.* It means trading a negative view for a positive view. In this case, facing your fear means you know you might lose your job, career, lifestyle, and economic base. Trust says *what is lost can be replaced.* Trust also affirms your ability to work out a new, exciting, and creative answer. There is a very challenging passage in Proverbs that speaks of trust: "Trust in the LORD with all your heart, / and do not rely on your own insight. / In all your ways acknowledge him, / and he will make straight your paths" (Prov. 3:5–6.)

The Fear of Moving in with Family

Moving closer to family members after divorce or the death of a fifty-something spouse is an option but also a fear. Many mothers and fathers who are invited to move in with their children soon discover the tremendous pressure on everyone involved. It is rare for a parent to live successfully with his or her adult children, and equally rare for a child to live successfully with the parent.

As much as possible, try to work out a detailed agreement with your child and his or her family before you make this change. Begin by asking yourself the following questions, adapted from *A Consumer's Guide to Aging*:

- Will I feel like a guest in my child's home?
- If my adult child lives far from my present residence, how will I maintain my friendships and other social contacts?
- What will loss of privacy and perhaps increased dependence mean for me?
- How will I handle conflicts in lifestyle and values?
- How will I contribute to family expenses?

Similarly, your adult child and his or her family should go through these questions before you move into their home:

- How will we maintain our lifestyle?
- What impact will this change have on the spouses and the children?

- What changes will our home need to accommodate an older relative?
- What contribution—financial or other—do I expect from my parent?
- What contribution do I need from other family members, such as my brothers and sisters?
- How will I handle conflicts and new demands on my time?[1]

Go through these lists separately. Then go through them together, working out answers that everyone can agree to.

Many single-again fifties people make other changes in where they live. I have watched many of them attempt to move "back home" where they grew up and where older parents and family members still reside. And a few months later I have watched them move back to the city they lived in while married. They soon discovered that home is where your most recent ties and friends are.

(In Chapter 10 we'll discuss a corollary of this situation: the fifty-something parents whose adult children move back in after a divorce.)

The Fear of Abusing Your Relationships

I personally wish more single-again people had this fear; it might help them avoid some of the pain and hurt they're prone to incur. Divorce and death leave painful scars on the heart, and it's natural to want to make that hurt go away. In our efforts to bring about healing, we turn to others to ease our pain. On a simple, caring level, there is nothing wrong with this, but we only get in trouble when we dump our entire load of hurts on another person and ask him or her to take responsibility for making them all go away. We are most vulnerable to abusing our relationships this way when our pain level is high and our self-esteem is low. Anyone who speaks a kind word to us is in danger of our load-dumping.

On the reverse side are those who prey on hurting people by offering their messianic services in exchange for having their needs met. These people take far more than they give, and they become abusers in the process. Hurting people will always have a high degree of vulnerability. Until their healing and self-confidence grow, they will be prime candidates for both inflicting and incurring relational abuse.

Fear of How the Loss Will Affect Loved Ones

One of the greatest fears at a time of loss is how that loss will impact other members of the family. This may be especially true when children are still living at home. And now that fathers and mothers going through a divorce are sometimes closely followed into divorce court by grandfathers and grandmothers, both children and grandchildren have become a prime concern in many cases. Their once-secure family structure can disappear overnight, ultimately to be replaced by a series of blended families.

After a divorce or the death of a spouse, be aware that your children may need more love than they did before. They also may need more quality time from you—and from your former spouse in the case of a divorce—especially if the children are not yet independent adults.

Many divorcing spouses in their fifties worry that their children—even adult children—will be hurt, angry, confused, or alienated by the parents' decision. And they're fearful about other kinds of impact as well, especially when adolescents or teenagers are involved. The statistics of crimes committed by children from broken homes is staggering, and too often children of divorced parents end up divorced, themselves, in their adult life.

Your children may benefit from the help of a counselor or other mental-health professional to help them navigate the turmoil surrounding death or divorce. Be ready to suggest or arrange that help if it is needed. The statistics of children who live through divorce and end up being healthy and successful in life are seldom displayed for all to see, but there are many of them. Nor do the success stories of single parents make news, but I have watched two decades of single parents around me do phenomenal jobs of child-rearing. They deserve gold stars and medals of valor.

Fear of Failure

The last item on my short list of common fears is fear of failure. Although this is something we all worry about from time to time, in the case of fifty-something singles, it is directly related to the fear of not being able to handle all the responsibilities they are left with after a death or divorce. This might include the wife who has never had any experience or training in dealing with the family's financial aspects or the husband who has no idea how to launder his clothes and choose patterns and colors of suits, shirts, and ties to portray a professional appearance. They worry that their inability to handle such basic responsibilities will mean life has lost its purpose for them.

Combine these fears together in one person and you have a potential major depression looming on the horizon. When a long-term marriage ends in a couple's fifties, fear says there are too many mountains to climb alone. But faith and trust counter by telling you that you can take your mountains one at a time, and with the help of God and a small army of friends you can climb them. I have listened to enough divorce-recovery stories over the years to know the mountains of fear can be conquered. I have watched people survive divorce or come back from the death of a spouse and climb out of the valley of their fears. It takes time and hard work, but it *can* happen.

One way you can identify and start resolving your fears is to write about them. The time-out exercise below, "Identifying, Confronting, and Resolving My Fears," can help you do this. First list all your fears about being single again at fifty-something in the left-hand column. Then think about each fear and, in the "Because" column, list what is causing it. Finally, in the "So now I will" column, write the action you can take to confront the fear, remove its source, or cope with it. If you can think of an alternative way to resolve the fear, write that in the right-hand column. I've developed one idea to get you started.

Identifying, Confronting, and Resolving My Fears About Being Single Again

I FEAR	BECAUSE	SO NOW I WILL	and (ALTERNATIVES)
Living alone	I may be harmed	Put in an alarm system	Tell my friends to call me once in a while
Living alone	It's too quiet	Buy a new stereo	_____

Never marrying again	I'm unattractive	Take a self-esteem course	
			————
————	————	————	————
————	————	————	————
————	————	————	————
————	————	————	————
————	————	————	————

List all YOUR fears and write in the things YOU can do to resolve them

The Three Stages of Recovery

In every traumatic life event, there are stages to the recovery process. If you know what they are, you can measure your growth and know you are on the road to wholeness.

Shock

Becoming single again at midlife leaves you with a seemingly bottomless hole in your life. At the moment of death or after a divorce, you stand in the first stage:

shock. In my book *Growing Through Divorce,* I explain shock this way:

> In a state of shock, people react in many different ways. Some retreat within themselves trying to block out all thoughts of what is happening. They choose to deny what is happening mentally and refuse to talk with anyone about it. They withdraw from friends and social contacts. Retreating sometimes turns into running. Inward feelings may run the gamut of personal guilt and failure to the transference of those feelings totally to another person.

You can exist in a state of shock for a long time. First there is an initial shock that numbs and paralyzes you. When that passes, it is often replaced by a dulling, emotional fog that can last for weeks. In this fog, logical thinking is substituted by irrational thinking, and emotional highs and lows become the order of the day.

Adjustment / Acceptance

Things begin to return to normal after a while, and shock is followed by a time of adjustment or acceptance. If we think of shock as a form of denial, we can describe adjustment as a form of integration. It is the stage of letting your life resume normal patterns and fitting your loss into those patterns. It is living out the decision to go on, one day at a time, and rejoin life and those around you. Grief and mourning are a vital part of any adjustment time. You need to reconnect with your feelings and express them as a part of this adjustment. Fears usually begin to spill out during this time, which generally takes up to a year after the loss is experienced. Gradually, self-confidence returns and life begins to fall into a pattern again.

Growth

The third stage of recovery usually clicks into gear in the second year. Growth means you start taking responsibility for yourself, you begin to set goals, and you make plans for *your* future. Growth is knowing you are making progress even if it is hard to measure. Growth is spending more time looking ahead of you than behind you. Growth is grand and glorious insecurity! Fear of the future is replaced by faith in the future. Then a new word sneaks into your vocabulary: *Freedom!*

Freedom says:

- I have choices.
- I can choose to do what I want.
- I have career and job options.
- I can continue my education.
- I can live wherever I choose.
- My choices are no longer contingent upon another person.
- I can stay out as late as I want at night.
- I can eat when I want and what I want.
- I can begin again.

Enjoying Life Again

When you suddenly become single again at fifty-something it is easy to become bitter and rage at life for its unfairness. I have talked with angry people who were divorced a year before retirement and had to watch as their former spouses moved into the retirement dream with someone else while the ones left behind were forced to look for a job.

"It's not fair!" they scream to all who will listen. No, it's not, and it never will be. But life will move on around you if you just sit there and scream. As long as you are alive, you have choices. Use your energy to pursue them instead of using your energy to stay angry.

It may take a while for you to fully realize that you now have these new choices, this new freedom. Many singles have told me they feel guilty when exercising these new freedoms for the first time. They feel they need someone to give them permission, but there is no longer anyone to ask. When they start dating, many say they feel like they are cheating on the former spouse. This is a strong feeling for the one whose mate has died and less troubling for those who have been divorced. For these reasons a few fifty-something people hesitate to make any choices at all.

It is hard to put to rest the memories, good and bad, and to move on with your life. Accepting new and personal challenges and forming new and supportive relationships takes time and a great deal of human energy. But people who find themselves alone again in their fifties are not losers in life—unless they choose to be.

Perhaps you feel you've been preparing for fifty years for the freedom and fun of this unique decade only to lose the one you wanted to share it with. You need to realize now that the preparation time is over and you have to make choices that will allow you to follow the dream for yourself. It may be different from the dream you shared with your spouse, but it can still be a very rewarding and satisfying adventure.

In my divorce-recovery seminars I often read one of two books to the participants. One is *The Little Engine That Could* and the other is *O, The Places You'll Go!* by Dr. Seuss. I recommend them to you too. Both send the powerful message that you can overcome obstacles and move ahead toward a future filled with unlimited possibilities.

Dr. Seuss's final word is: "So . . . get on your way!"

7

Surviving a Midlife Crisis

It is not a question of how a husband and wife can be equal and alike. But rather a problem of how a couple can be equal and different.
Pierre Mornell

THERE IS A great line in the film *Middle-Age Crazies*. As a man drives his older sister to the airport she babbles on and on about her troubles and how unfair life has been to her. As the man peers out at life through a rain-spattered windshield, he suddenly starts to mumble the words, "I don't want to be the daddy anymore!" All the people in his world—wife, kids, older parents, older sister, and even his employees—look to him as the "daddy." He is tired of being everyone's daddy, and he wants to run away. All of a sudden he echoes the cry that many of us have silently restrained through the years. We don't want to be the daddy (or mommy) anymore.

There are probably very few fifty-something folks who did not want to leave it all behind and run away at least a few times in their lives. Those who give in to this urge are said to be having a midlife crisis.

For many years, the midlife crisis was the exclusive domain of men. Typically, they lived out their "crises" in this scenario: Midlife man dumps wife and family and runs off with twenty-three-year-old secretary. Prior to or during this sidebar in his life, midlife man started dressing in younger and more trendy clothes, traded in his Oldsmobile Ninety-Eight for a Mercedes 560SL convertible, and joined a health club. Everyone in midlife man's life declared him in crisis and desperately sought to find a logical reason for his latent attempt to be twenty-something again. Job stress, a fading of youth, marriage problems, and poor self-esteem were only a few of the designated culprits blamed for the crisis.

Today increasing numbers of women in this age group are following in their male predecessors' footsteps, leaving husbands stranded as they initiate divorces, career changes, affairs, and new lifestyles.

"How Could This Happen?"

The term *midlife crisis* has been used to describe any unusual or abnormal behavior that occurs in a man or woman between the ages of forty and sixty. Some refer to it only as a crisis of personality precipitated by rapid and substantial changes in personal behavior. However it is defined, in its 1990s version midlife crisis impacts entire family systems. Long-term marriages of thirty and forty years are falling victim to this life-shaking dilemma as it plows through the entire fifty-something decade.

From a purely human perspective, we could isolate fifteen or twenty things that contribute to the midlife crisis. The ones that appear most frequently are:

- Lack of communication.
- Lack of affection.
- Financial stress and strain.

- Lack of creative goals.
- Lack of quality time together.
- Unrealistic expectations of the marriage or the spouse.

But identifying all the contributors to a midlife crisis doesn't alleviate the problem; nor does it firmly answer how a person can seem to change so dramatically and move into a new lifestyle without missing a beat. I have had hundreds of people tell me that their midlife-crisis spouse is now a total stranger to them. A midlife crisis changes a person so completely that those who thought they knew him or her best suddenly don't feel they know the person even remotely.

The fallout in decimated family structures is enormous, and the children in those families may grow up only to duplicate what they experienced in their family of origin. If a father or mother can have an affair in midlife that ends a thirty-year marriage, what's wrong with a child later duplicating the process in his or her own marriage? When examples of strength are removed from the life of a child, they are usually replaced by examples of weakness and fear.

In a midlife crisis both men and women can abandon entire families to be with another person. In many instances all contact with family members is broken. So not only does the left-behind wife or husband feel deserted, but children, grandchildren, sisters, brothers, and a network of relatives may also fall victim to midlife crises.

On the other extreme of total family abandonment, there are those who want their primary families to accept their new situation and pretend that nothing has happened. A new husband, wife, or "significant other" is introduced as a new player in the family, and everyone is to pretend that nothing has changed.

I watch this dynamic played out in about 70 percent of all midlife crises that end up in divorce. Some children and other family members merely yawn and go on their way while others continue to be filled with rage, anger, and revenge.

While a midlife crisis does have some positive potential, it typically leaves more victims than victors in its wake. Unfortunately, those who are going through the crisis seldom stop long enough to add up what they will win in the short run versus what they will lose in the long run. They make instant decisions that will have a lifelong impact on the people involved.

A midlife crisis doesn't always focus on a new relationship. Many people have told me they just "don't want to be married any longer," or they wanted to be alone to pursue whatever lifestyle options came along. No other man or woman was waiting in the wings for them; they just wanted their freedom. This is hard for the left-behind person to accept and believe because the first question everyone asks is "Who is it?" It may be more of a personal put-down to be left for no one than to be left for someone.

Either way, the crisis of midlife claims its victims.

The Emotions of Midlife Crisis

What are people feeling emotionally when they are moving toward or caught in a midlife crisis? After twenty years of working in this area, I would say the primary emotions are fear and rejection.

The **fear** inherent in a midlife crisis is usually expressed around a number of inner questions:

1. Is this all there is to my life?
2. Am I missing something that would make me happier than I am?
3. What if I don't grab at this new opportunity? Will I have regrets the rest of my life?
4. Is there a better person out there for me than the one I now have?
5. Will being with a younger person make me feel younger?
6. Will my freedom really make me a free person?

I believe all these questions and many more haunt the inner spirit at midlife. And even though they are based on fear, these questions are quite real to the person who's feeling them. As long as they remain unanswered, this person is vulnerable to allowing someone else to become the "answer" to his or her personal quandaries.

The tragedy of a midlife crisis that ends in divorce is that the person in the crisis appears to have found an answer while the spouse who is left behind has no answers at all. One person appears to move toward a new sunrise in life while the sun seems to be setting for the rejected person. And the unhappiness is not limited to the spouse and family left behind. *Initiators of a midlife crisis always appear to be the winners on the surface but a few years down the road, they may be tragic losers in another divorce.*

The person who is left behind in the crisis will initially

feel overwhelmed by **rejection.** To live is to experience rejection in many forms, but somehow it is always most painful for those who are very human. The longer we live and feel accepted, the tougher it is to handle rejection when it comes. Rejection can only be replaced by acceptance, and that may take a very long time to achieve. Rejection pulls the rug of affirmation out from under us and sends the message that we are not adequate, not good enough.

Many marriages that collapse in the fifty-something years were good marriages until a year or two before the midlife crisis in one partner. The upsetting and unanswered thought for many is, *How could thirty good years be traded overnight for whatever or whomever?* On the surface, it doesn't look like a very good trade, but *in a crisis people tend to gamble rather than work from logic, reason, and reality.*

Escaping from Responsibility

The thought that stops most of us from giving in to the urges of a midlife crisis is *Responsible people don't run from their problems; they face them and conquer them.* I agree. Suppressed feelings about the problems and events in our lives can take on a life of their own and eventually surface with devastating results.

Fifty-something is a time for reducing some responsibilities and the shifting of others—or it can be a phase when you try to make up for lost time and opportunities. For example, married children can exert more pressure on you than you ever dreamed possible. When I started writing this book several months ago, my wife and I were living four hundred miles down Interstate 10 from our three children. Our lives were relatively free from any pressures from them. All of that changed dramatically when one child and her two children experienced financial struggles and moved two miles away from us. Little did we realize that all her pressures would become a daily part of our existence. We have discovered the easy problems that we once helped her solve have been replaced by tough ones that may go unresolved for many months.

Many men and women caught in a midlife crisis are struggling with the responsibility issue. "Tired out," "burned out," and "bored to death" describe many of these men and women. The tragedy is that many of them have been living in dead marriages that have long needed vital resuscitation. When that does not occur, one partner or the other may look for an exit.

Can Midlife Crisis Be Prevented?

Many people are lucky enough to escape midlife crises in any form; they wonder what all the fuss is about.

Other fifty-something people experience a midlife crisis—but try to deny or conceal it.

I believe many midlife crises would either never happen or find resolution if we could honestly get in touch with our feelings, find the right place to express them, and explore ways to resolve them—in short, if we could be honest with ourselves and our loved ones.

That honesty is very important during our fifties when we start adding up our wins and losses. We have to be honest with the results, acknowledging feelings and fears that have been buried beneath years of protective coating. This may especially be true among devoutly religious persons who have been told to trust God, deny feelings, and not ask questions. To wrestle with realities was said to be unspiritual. Real Christians were just not supposed to have problems, so denying them became a way of life.

When we are faced with radical reexamination at any place in our lives, we have to own our questions and process them with trusted friends or counselors. Many fifty-something men on the edge of midlife crisis have talked freely about their feelings to me but have never mentioned word one to anyone else. The male spirit tends to protect others from painful struggles they might face while drowning in those struggles themselves. In contrast, the female spirit is far more free in speaking out about thoughts, feelings, and questions. Men live behind the protective shield of vocation while women live more open to the relational aspects of life. However, both sexes can still bottle up feelings for years without giving them honest release. The result is emotional indigestion that often erupts in a midlife crisis involving another person.

Midlife Crises and Careers

Midlife crises can send men and women in opposite directions. While a man in midlife crisis may seek a new relationship, a common component of a woman's midlife crisis is seeking a new role—switching careers or exchanging her role as full-time wife and mother to become a student or enter the job market. The woman may be seeking a greater identity and sense of mastery and control over her life through a vocation while the opposite situation may push a fifty-something man into midlife crisis. Boredom with a career that offers no challenge or opportunity for further advancement can cause the man to dream of other possibilities for this portion of his life; it can also cause him to look for fulfillment in affairs, drugs, alcohol, and gambling—the most common boredom fillers.

It may be easier for a woman to start a new life in the work force at fifty-something than it is for a man to quit a career and look for new options. The woman's choice is an exciting challenge in pursuit of new growth. As she starts a new career, she builds new relationships in the work place that have the potential to replace the role of her spouse. Meanwhile, just the opposite is happening to the husband who, as part of his midlife crisis, quits his job and finds himself suddenly unappreciated (at least professionally) and alone at home during the day. This can plunge the man into a deep depression while the woman is becoming euphoric.

I have watched these dynamics played out in scores of lives in the past ten years. If these feelings are not addressed and understood by both people, the spouses will become increasingly distant from each other in every area of meaning. (We'll discuss the issue of fifty-something job and career loss in more detail in the next chapter.)

Communicating about the Crisis

Realizing that they are at a midlife turning point, many fifty-something spouses *want* to communicate about these issues, but they've forgotten *how* (if they ever really knew). If that's your situation, you may find it helpful to use the checklists below as a starting point for being honest with each other about your midlife fears and feelings. Each spouse completes his or her checklist, marking the statements that apply. Then the two of you take a time-out to discuss your responses and your options for dealing with them. Make sure there are no distractions: turn off the television and put down the newspaper. Discuss your responses and your feelings clearly and listen with your heart. Repeat back to your spouse, in your own words, what you heard him or her say so you both agree on what is being expressed.

A Time-Out to Look at the Common Disparities between Men and Women's Fears and Feelings at Midlife

Men

_____ 1. I may be in danger of losing a job.

_____ 2. I am in the midst of the most job stress I've ever had.

_____ 3. I might try an affair to prove something.

_____ 4. I may not even notice the children have left home since work relationships continue as usual.

_____ 5. I may be glad the children have gone so that increased job responsibilities can be done at home at night.

_____ 6. I may be looking and feeling much older.

_____ 7. I may be feeling rejected at work and home.

_____ 8. I may feel unimportant and obsolete.

_____ 9. I may be wondering why God doesn't seem to be taking care of things.

_____ 10. I may not want to talk to anyone about what's happening because this would only show more failure.

———— 11. I may be trying to reduce my responsibilities due to self-doubts or job burn-out.

———— 12. I may try to use "fillers" (drugs, gambling, sex) to take my mind off a failing career.

———— 13. I may be hard to understand and relate to due to all the negative changes I'm enduring.

———— 14. I may be living in denial.

———— 15. I may be feeling suicidal at times.

Women

———— 1. I may be getting the opportunity to (re)start a career.

———— 2. I may have the most rewarding job feelings I've ever had.

———— 3. I may try an affair with someone who understands and accepts my new career and lifestyle.

———— 4. I may really be missing the children and have few if any adult relationships to replace them.

———— 5. I may feel relieved but miss the responsibility of caring for children.

———— 6. I may be feeling and looking younger due to children gone.

———— 7. I may feel accepted, important, and reborn in a new career.

———— 8. I may be totally depressed with nothing to do and no one to talk to at home.

———— 9. I may be excited and wondering where God is leading me.

———— 10. I may be willing to share with everyone all the new and exciting things that are happening.

———— 11. I may use "fillers" (alcohol, drugs, gambling, sex) to fill empty time at home.

_____ 12. I may find it hard to understand both the positive and negative changes.

_____ 13. I may be hard to understand and relate to due to all the negative changes I'm enduring.

A Doorway to Growth

Any midlife crisis can become a doorway to further growth if we are willing to face it honestly, talk it through with the people involved, and develop a positive plan of action. A healthy part of that plan would be to seek the help of a competent counselor or therapist. Remember, asking for help is a sign of strength, not weakness. Refusing to face the experience inwardly or outwardly will not cause it to disappear; nothing ever gets resolved by denying its existence.

A midlife crisis is one more stop on the road of life's transitions. It can be a place of disaster, or it can be a positive intersection where we reevaluate past accomplishments and disappointments, assess present and future opportunities, and experience new growth.

Here are fifteen suggestions to help you deal effectively with a midlife crisis:

1. Admit it is a real-life event in some people's lives and can be very real in yours.
2. Realize it can happen to anybody, anywhere, at any time. Being a strong person spiritually does not exempt you.
3. Write down the feelings and thoughts you are experiencing. Keep a notebook or journal handy so they don't escape you.
4. Begin talking through your feelings and thoughts

with your spouse, a few trusted friends, or a counselor.

5. Try to identify where your feelings of crisis are coming from: past, present, or future.

6. Find a competent counselor or therapist who can help you explore in depth what you are going through.

7. Read books and other literature that can give insight into your situation.

8. Don't pretend everything is all right when you know it isn't.

9. Try to find a few other people who have been where you are and can share how they processed their midlife crisis in a positive way. Stay away from those who have handled it the wrong way.

10. Understand that these things happen in the lives of good people.

11. Know that you are still normal if it happens to you but to no one else around you. We all tend to check our normalcy by reflecting our experience in the mirror of another person's life.

12. Understand that a midlife crisis usually begins with a conspiracy of jumbled feelings that make little or no sense to you.

13. Understand that a midlife crisis can be prompted by events that were beyond your control.

14. Allow yourself a solid block of time to work through a midlife crisis. Resist quick solutions and deal with the realities of what can be gained and what can be lost forever by the choices you make.

15. Ask for God's help and guidance. People experiencing a midlife crisis are as loved by God as those who are not.

If you are facing some of the feelings and issues we have talked about in this chapter, get the help you need to weather the storm. Regardless of what those around you may think, a midlife crisis is more than a pothole in your road through life. It is real. And without positive intervention, it can be disastrous to your loved ones—and to you.

8

Beginning Again
When a Career Ends

*Losses happen across the life span, but they take
on a special meaning during mid-life. People are
in the process of evaluating their lives. They are
beginning to give different meanings to family,
work, and themselves. A recognition and
acceptance of the finiteness of time causes part of
this change. They are more aware that they will
die. Some of the major losses incurred in mid-life
involve work, family, and personal life.*

Shirley A. Waskel
Mid-Life Issues and the Workplace of the '90s

ELIZABETH ABRAMS HAD started with Barrington
Transportation, Inc., as a telemarketer right after she
graduated from college. The pay was low and it seemed
there was little chance of her ever moving beyond a sales
rep because of the "good ole boy" system that was well in
place.

But Elizabeth was determined, and she was in a good
place to learn the business. After a year, she went back to
school on nights and weekends to get her MBA. She continued working with Barrington, moving up to a sales rep
position.

When she completed her MBA, Elizabeth landed a position in Barrington's marketing/advertising division. She

was there for the long haul, committed to the company, loyal to those with whom she worked. Elizabeth continued working with Barrington through her marriage and the educating of her three children. She was repeatedly promoted, first to assistant manager, then manager of marketing.

As she approached her fifty-second year, Elizabeth had practically been guaranteed a promotion to vice president —the first woman ever named vice president at Barrington. Instead, the company offered her early retirement in an unexpected effort to cut back.

Thirty years of loyalty and labor, ready to be a vice president, and Elizabeth was out of work. How could she face her friends? What would she do?

The Times, They Are a Changin'

Losing a job or a career at midlife was seldom thought about before the 1980s. Then, toward the end of that decade, the entire world cycled into a dramatic change. Walls went down and war machines began dismantling. Segments of our tried-and-true financial structure in America began collapsing and economic hard times touched the untouchable.

The widest swathe of all job loss in this area has cut through the fifty-something decade. The Bureau of Labor Statistics shows that from October 1991 to October 1992 the unemployment rate in those aged fifty-five and older was seven times that of those aged sixteen to fifty-four.[1] The middle-management age group, which was once considered most secure and which consists primarily of people in the fifty-something decade, has been particularly hard hit. A recent article titled "Downward Mobility" in *Business Week* said, "Since the mid-1980's, as corporations have responded to global competition and technological change by merging and consolidating, downsizing and de-layering, some 2 million middle management positions have been permanently eliminated."

Thus, in a few short years, millions of men (and also women, to a lesser extent) fell from the height of their careers into the depths of despair. The fifty-something people who had been looking forward to their fifties as a time of power, success, and financial security suddenly found themselves filled with fear and worry as they scrambled to reshuffle their dreams. One fifty-something manager in a large worldwide company described this situation when he said, "When I finally got to the party, I found it was over . . . and I had no place else to go."

Losing a Job Means Losing an Identity

Losing a job or terminating a career has a powerful impact on our personal identity. Much of the time, we are what we do vocationally. When we meet a new person our most common question is usually "What do you do?" Our response to that person is conditioned by his or her answer.

While she was employed by Barrington Elizabeth was the life of the party, welcoming people to her community and establishing contacts for them. After she lost her job, she lost her sense of purpose and place within her circle of friends. She could no longer introduce herself to newcomers as "Elizabeth Abrams, manager of sales and advertising at Barrington." She had little to say when friends asked her how her day had been.

You can watch the difference in people's reactions

when you tell them you are unemployed and when you tell them you are Dr. So-and-So. What we do or do not do job-wise impresses or "unimpresses" the people we meet. Apparently it also impresses us because we tend to talk a lot about what we do. In effect we are saying, "This is what I do. I'm important!"

When we lose a job or career, we may have trouble convincing others we are still important. A large part of our identity is quickly lost, and we are left asking ourselves, "Who am I now?"

Feelings That Accompany Job and Career Loss

Losing something as valuable as a career can bring many other emotions into play besides grief. They can strike in an instant and immobilize you for the rest of the day or week. Some of the common feelings I see people expressing in this area are: *fear and panic, denial and blame, anger, depression,* and *loss of self-worth and self-esteem.* Any one of these alone is a challenge to overcome. When all of them are unleashed on you at the same time, they become debilitating. Your choice is either "fight or flight," and you may have to make this choice every day. One day, you take a stand and decide to face your feelings and fight through them. On another day, you want to run as far away as you can.

One of the questions looming largest on the horizon when these emotions surround you is, "Does everyone else feel like I do? Is this normal?" This is one of the keys to processing feelings: having them validated by others. This validation will not change what you are feeling, but it will tell you it is OK to have those feelings and you are not alone.

Validation is my goal in describing these common emotions here in a little more detail. When you recognize them in yourself you can be assured that you are not the only one who has these feelings after a job or career loss.

Fear and Panic

In a fifty-something job loss, fear can control a person to the point of panic, rendering him or her immobile. In my experience the three greatest fears involved in a job loss are the fear of failure, the fear of the future with all its uncertainties, and the fear of what those around you, both family and friends, will think of you in your loss.

Fear is usually removed when trust is restored, and trust is restored by rebuilding self-worth and self-esteem. Fear can also be removed by taking positive action now about what you fear may happen later. Fear says *What if?* while trust says *I can*. A friend of mine says, "Fear is knowing you are in charge. Trust is knowing that God is in charge!" This poem by Thomas Merton says it so well:

> My Lord God,
> I have no idea
> where I am going.
> I do not see the road
> ahead of me. I cannot
> know where it will end.
> Nor do I really know myself,
> and the fact that I think that
> I am following your will does
> not mean that I actually
> am doing so. But I believe
> that the desire to please you
> does in fact please you.

And I hope I have that desire
in all I am doing. I hope
that I will never do anything
apart from that desire. And
I know that if I do this, you
will lead me by the right road
though I may know nothing about
it. Therefore, I will trust you
always though I may seem to be
lost in the shadow of death.
I will not fear for you are ever
with me, and you will never
leave me to face my perils alone.

The deadliest thing about fear is that it can immobilize us from taking any action on our situation. It can also be passed along to family members until an entire household is paralyzed. For some people who are recovering from a job or career loss, fear is the emotion that must be fought and conquered every day. It may help to remember that about 90 percent of what we fear most never happens. That should tell us something about the amount of energy and time we should give to our greatest fears.

When we are so overwhelmed with everything that we are either numbed totally or we say and do erratic things that only make our situation worse, we have been seized by panic. Panic says *There is no way I can control anything. I will be consumed by everything!* Panic is our rational sense becoming irrational.

Panic hits most often when we are alone. Some people live with "panic attacks" as a part of their life but learn through therapy how to control them. One of the best ways to deal with situational panic is to find some calm and gentle friends to talk with. Voices of hope and sanity around us can go a long way in helping navigate the seas of panic. While panic might say there is no way out, our friends and support systems can take our hand and lead us to a more peaceful place.

Denial and Blame

Elizabeth Abrams became an expert at denial and blame after she lost her job at Barrington. "I'll just give this a few weeks," she'd tell herself in the quiet of her home. "This won't last long. They'll get over some financial hump they've run into and call me back in a few months."

But a few weeks passed and then a few months, and no calls. And as Elizabeth sat at home alone, her bitterness began to grow. First, she blamed the company for her loss.

Of course, Elizabeth thought, *Barrington can hire two or three people, just out of college, to do what I was doing. And they'll get by with paying less to all of those kids than they paid to me alone. Whatever happened to "last hired, first fired"?*

Despite the fact that several men had also been laid off, Elizabeth began to think the company just had something against women. She had been insistent through the years about leaving the office on time so she could be with her family. She had children and wanted to be home in time to prepare their supper and talk with them about their day. She speculated that upper management had resented this or thought she should have worked overtime. She even felt some resentment toward her husband and children, thinking perhaps they had held her back.

When you lose a job or career in the middle of your

life, you can indulge in denial all you want, pretending the job loss doesn't bother you. And when you are fearful and full of self-doubts, you can deny them by trying to hide them. But in either case, the basic problems and feelings will not go away. You will not grow beyond them until you deal with them by acceptance and admission.

I have a wonderful coffee mug in my office that I usually place in the middle of my desk when I am counseling. It says, "Denial Is Not a River in Egypt!" Many of the people I counsel are denial experts who have practiced the fine art for years. Denial says, *What's happening is not happening and if I deny it's happening, it will go away!* Reality, on the other hand, says, *What's happening is happening and I had better do something about it.*

We learn the art of denial when we're very young. We tell our parents we will not be afraid when they turn our bedroom light out at night, and we tell ourselves we won't be afraid. But they turn out the light and leave, and we are afraid. We start pretending that if we deny our fear it will go away and life will go on. If we deal with all our fearful issues that way, by the time we reach fifty-something, we become denial experts.

Blame is a form of deflected denial; it admits a problem exists but says it was created by others. It sometimes seems that blaming each other has become our national pastime. At moments of loss, we all look for someone to blame. This started as far back as the Garden of Eden when Eve blamed the serpent. Author John Powell says, "Blaming is a game. It removes me from reality. Blaming is essentially a way of shifting responsibility and maintaining power over others. Growth begins where blaming ends." No one wins the blame game. The best advice here is "let it go!" It doesn't really matter who is at fault.

Anger

I have had many people tell me they have a right to be angry and to stay angry after they've lost their careers. I do not deny that right. If your company dismisses you after twenty-four years of faithful service with a six-month severance package and a pat on the back, you have a right to be angry. To stay angry for the next six months, though, will not help you get on with your life's journey in a healthy way. It takes great energy to stay angry, and you could better use that energy to regroup, retrain, and rethink the rest of your life. Although anger has some positive sides to it, much of what we direct to others only steals something from us that we cannot afford to give.

Depression

Depression turns our feelings inward and suffocates our spirit. It is both the outward and inward act of feeling sorry for ourselves. After Jerry was laid off from his company at the age of fifty-one, he spent most of his time at home, watching TV. "Early retirement," he called it when friends stopped him on his occasional trip to the store and asked him what he was doing these days. But if he cornered you at a party, all Jerry talked about was the disloyalty and greed of corporate America. "You'd never believe what they did to me," Jerry would say. "Early retirement, my eye!"

Jerry was keeping his depression alive by telling everyone he met what a bad deal he got from his company. When we do the same, with each telling of the story, we add fuel to the depression. It doesn't take long before we are emotionally strangled.

Depression is always seeing the negative side of every situation. Depression is also the grave that many of these emotions and feelings will plunge us into if they are not processed and resolved.

Rebuilding Your Life after a Career Loss

Many fifty-something people who fall victim to these feelings and responses after a job loss are able to work through them in a healthy way so they can move on to new growth in their lives. Others fall into a holding pattern, fearful of making any moves or decisions lest they make the wrong ones. They float for months in a stagnant zone, unable to move ahead. They build a memorial to what they once did but no longer do. It is easy to become comfortable in this holding pattern, but it's not productive. Memories need to be filed away and the doors to yesterday have to be closed so new windows of opportunity can open.

The following section will give you ideas of some positive steps you can take to begin a new life following the loss of a job or a career at fifty-something. Be aware that the recovery process may occur over several weeks or months. It will not be accomplished overnight. In an article for *Modern Maturity* called "How to Find a Job," Diane Herz of the Bureau of Labor Statistics was quoted, saying that the median time for people fifty-five to sixty-four to find a new job was twice as long, 16.7 weeks, as that for people aged sixteen to fifty-four, 8.8 weeks. There could be various reasons for this, of course. People at age fifty-five to sixty-four may take longer to find another job because they are overqualified for most jobs or they are experiencing discrimination. But they may also be taking more time because they have pensions and savings that can support them while they look.[2]

Talk about It

I have watched too many husbands and even a few wives try to protect their families from sharing the pain and uncertainty caused by job and career loss. The standard line to spouses and children is, "Don't worry; everything will be fine and this won't change a thing for you."

Assuring maybe. Dishonest, definitely!

The best way to cope with job loss is to involve your family in your journey back to a full life. In essence you ask them to help you set up a "Family Response and Action Plan" through frequent and honest discussions. Normal, healthy children of almost all ages can usually handle truth very well, and they can actually give strong, outstanding support in its wake. If family is anything, it should be a team, and when one team member is in trouble, the team should have the opportunity to rally around and give support in any and all areas.

And there's another aspect to this honesty: Children watching their fifty-something parents cope successfully with this kind of life change will learn how to handle transitions so that their own changes in later life will not destroy them.

When you discuss the situation with your family, talk about the positives and the negatives, the knowns and the unknowns, so that everything is revealed for all to understand and there are no hidden secrets and no false promises. Keep family members constantly updated on your progress, both victories and defeats. Talk through all the options as well as how each one would affect the family members.

One of the real keys in involving family members is to let them respond to anything by stating how they *feel*. Too often feelings are bottled up inside, creating a volatile home atmosphere just waiting to explode.

Remember that your spouse needs to be an intricate part of your struggle as well as the possible solution. An informed spouse can be a tremendous support in the form of a cheerleader, encourager, confidante, and catalyst. On the other hand, an uninformed spouse ends up playing the role of critic, complainer, and distracter.

Even when the family is informed and involved, as the days of unemployment lengthen and the financial resources dwindle, tremendous tension can build. Tomorrow is looked upon as offering more struggles than strength. A family that once felt upwardly mobile now realizes it is downwardly fragile. Harsh words take the place of gentle encouragement and all nine innings of the blame game are played out daily. If this happens, family members may isolate themselves from each other, causing communication to break down. Family strength is severely tested in such crises. Many divorces today are the result of job or career loss. Many would never have happened if the family had pulled together instead of pulling each other apart.

We could learn a great deal today by watching reruns of "The Waltons" and "Little House on the Prairie." The resounding theme in both those former prime-time television series was commitment to the family. When crises arose, the family was involved in the problem as well as the solution. Family values were placed above family conflicts. We would do well today to take a side trip now and then to Walton's Mountain and learn how to remove some of our own mountains.

Talk Resources, Not Problems

In our society we have more resources to cope with job loss than ever before, and the quality of these resources and the help they can provide are awesome. Most are just a phone call away. But people who have spent years in management are accustomed to *giving* help, not asking for it. After a humiliating job loss there is enough pride in most of us to keep us away from those who could help us recover.

It is easier to spend our time talking about our problems than to tap into available resources for overcoming it. We know our problems so well that it takes little effort to pass them along to all we meet. Some people who do this think they are networking when in reality they are complaining.

Several groups around the country have emerged as valuable networking resources for job hunters in their fifty-something years. Organizations like the Five O'Clock Club in Manhattan and Forty Plus in Washington, D.C., as well as other cities, charge weekly fees to join and hear lectures, receive résumé critiques, form strategy groups that brainstorm ideas for each person's next step in his or her job hunt, and learn new interview techniques. Operation ABLE, in Chicago, is a nonprofit organization that specializes in employment and training programs. And the AARP has its own eight-part employment program available for thirty-five dollars. Find out if your community has a similar organization, or start one of your own.

Use the library and your local bookstores to research

job-hunting techniques and new business options. *Mid-Career Job Hunting: Official Handbook of the 40+* Club by E. Patricia Birsner (Simon & Schuster/ARCO, 1991) and *The Over-40 Job Guide* by Kathryn and Ross Petras (Simon and Schuster/Poseidon, 1993) can give you some practical tips in a search for a new job.

You also may have a skill from your former employment you could use in starting your own business. If you worked on a production team with a publishing company, for example, research starting your own desktop publishing business out of your home. If you worked with a company whose headquarters was overseas or one that specialized in oil or large machinery, learn what you can about starting an import/export business. Search the library for information on small businesses. Several magazines also offer insight into starting your own business out of your home. Call your local Better Business Bureau to see if they can recommend how to order some of these.

Remember that focusing on problems will deter you from talking about resources and solutions. As the old philosopher remarked, "You are either a part of the problem or a part of the solution." Identify and keep a working list of all available resources as you rebuild your life in the areas of job or career loss. Answers and help often come from strange places as well as from recognized sources. Check out all of them. Most importantly, do not be afraid to ask for help. People will not know your needs unless you tell them.

Tap into a Community of Faith

The gift of faith comes to many of us through other people. When our own faith is weak, we need a community of faith and love around us to nourish us. For many people, that is a church family. For others it might be a service club, a hobby group, people in our neighborhood, or a support group composed of people in situations similar to our own. These groups give us an instant identity with fellow strugglers plus a cheerleading squad when we need one.

The story of a man in one such group appeared in *Modern Maturity*. Ron Rich, a Denver participant in AARP WORKS, a training and networking group, said, "When we were discussing our experience [one gentleman in our class said], 'You know, there's enough talent in this class to start a corporation.' It gave us the extra oomph we needed to stick in there and see what we could do."[2] Burdens shared are burdens lifted; faith shared is strength received.

There are three embracing faith circles in our lives: faith in God, faith in ourselves, and faith in others. When a crisis like job or career loss hits, it shakes our faith and tests its strength. When it happens in the fifty-something decade, one can feel that all three faith circles have disappeared completely. Unemployment can instantly kill the faith you had in your former company and its leaders, the faith you had in yourself to do the job, and the belief you had in your gifts, talents, and abilities. Left only with a shaky faith in God, the question becomes, "Where is God in all this, and does He really care?"

A strong community of supportive friends is always the foundation for rebuilding faith, but even then, lost faith in any area cannot be restored overnight. When our faith is inoperative, we need to see it operating in others. When it is absent, we need others to have faith for us.

Over my own lifetime when my faith was lagging it was always important for me to know that I could call some friends and ask them to have faith for me. Without that knowledge, I don't know where I would be today.

Don't Spend Too Much Time Alone

There are many lone-ranger people who are quick to tell us they don't need anyone to help them handle their struggles. Perhaps their trust in others was betrayed and now they are convinced they must "go it alone."

People who grew up in homes where they were taught to be self-sufficient and never ask anyone for help tend to be loners. The thought of sharing hopes, fears, and dreams with another person is completely foreign to them. Whatever mountains they face, they are convinced they must climb them alone. This means they frequently exclude family as well as friends. These are loners by choice, and many of them will remain so throughout life.

A second group of loners is set apart by their experience. Where they once were a part of a functioning group of employed people, they are now distanced by their loss of employment. They feel no sense of belonging to anything viable and choose to suffer in emotional and social isolation. When their career resumes, they click back into a relational gear and go on with life.

Being alone too much can readily become destructive. Some who tend to be alone feel they are unworthy failures and no one would want to be with them. On the other extreme, some feel they are too good to be with fellow strugglers. Let's hope there are more people in the middle of these two groups than at the opposite ends!

After a job loss, don't spend too much time alone. We all need the understanding, camaraderie, and undergirding of others when our only employment is rebuilding our lives.

Read Positive, Growth-Producing Materials

Ron Rich, the Denver participant in AARP WORKS I mentioned earlier, had retired at age fifty-two from his position as an elementary schoolteacher and principal because of stress. Having been in education for most of his life, he felt there was nothing else he could do and feared looking for another job. But he finally decided to take action.

Ron enrolled in the AARP WORKS employment program in Denver and at the same time started a newsletter, "Booktalk," related to children's books and aimed at librarians and teachers.

The self-examinations administered at the Works program had revealed that Ron had a strong interest in children's books. So he created a program called "Let's Read a Book" that sends him into elementary schools to act out his favorite books for children. The program has triple benefits, he said. "I charge a fee, it motivates the youngsters to read, and it's fun."

Just as Ron was completing the employment program, he saw a job advertised with a Barnes & Noble bookstore. He interviewed and got the job. Six months later, the bookstore promoted him to children's book specialist.

Now Rich makes money from all of his ventures—the newsletter, the school program, and the bookstore. He is doing something he loves—working with children's books—and has escaped the pressures of being a principal.[3]

Positive messages in any form are life builders. Negative messages are life disablers. It is far more life-enhancing to spend time with positive people, like Ron Rich, and positive reading materials. When we are wallowing in our personal sea of despair, we need to grab hold of every positive thought we can.

I frequently send struggling people to a local bookstore to load up with positive reading such as books by Norman Vincent Peale and Robert Schuller. Magazines such as *Modern Maturity* also contain inspiring stories of people who have successfully made it through tough times.

When we think we can't do something, we need to be told we can by those who already have. If you spend all your time listening to gloomy economic forecasts and rising unemployment figures, you will definitely want to hide out under your bed for the next five years. Resist the negative and embrace the positive.

Keep a Daily Journal

Keeping a daily record of your journey back from a career loss will allow you to measure your progress and growth. It will also become a permanent record of your victories, your defeats, and your feelings each day. We can only measure our growth if we have a yardstick, and a journal is a tool to help do that. Years later, if another job crisis hits your life, you can go back and read about how you got through the last one. Be sure to list the various people who walked with you and what their contributions were on your journey. The way we handle our adversity becomes both an inspiration and a guide to those who follow behind.

Empowering Yourself after a Career Loss

To be cast adrift on the sea of unemployment at twenty- or thirty-something is not quite as life-threatening as it is at fifty-something. When you lose your career in your fifties, it may mean that for the rest of your life you'll have a very different career—or no career, if you choose to retire. In confronting this change, a great part of the empowering of fifty-something people is embracing a whole new challenge, a dramatic new lifestyle, a reevaluation of priorities, values, and standards, and perhaps a new geographical home. By responding this way your crisis can be renamed as "redirection" and "exploring new opportunities."

Things will not be the same, and you will have to find a new way to adapt to the changes. Here are some thoughts to remember as you continue your journey when faced with a life change:

When I have fears . . .
I will not let them immobilize me and I will trust God to be in charge.

When I panic . . .
I will not lose control. I will seek out friends, support systems, and help.

When I slip into denial . . .
I will not allow myself to linger there, and I will accept my realities and move forward.

When I want to blame others . . .
I will not blame anyone, including myself. I will recognize that blaming is a game that produces no winners.

When I am angry . . .

I will not be forced to agree that wrong is right and I will become rational so that I can deal responsibly with my anger.

When I am depressed . . .

I will not try to deny it or hide it. I will let others help me decide what my next steps are.

When I lose self-esteem . . .

I will not accept rejection or reject acceptance, and I will bounce back.

9

Outsmarting the Retirement Myth

Retirement is part of the myth of success in America . . . and few people stop to think of its deleterious consequences.

Steve Berglas

IN MY GROWING-UP years, I never heard my farming relatives talk of retiring or leaving the farm. Back then, America was primarily an agrarian society, and all hands, young and old, shared the farming workload. Most people expected to work throughout their entire lives until their health failed and their work had to be reduced or terminated. Farmers were farmers until they died.

Things are different now. As the winds of change blew across the farmlands of America, mechanization gave birth to factories and industries within our cities. People were no longer living in the midst of their work; they went somewhere else to do their jobs. Eventually they were told that someday they could quit working and live off the money that the government took from their weekly paychecks.

Until the advent of the social security system, retiring was almost unknown as an option for later life. With the first wave of retirees to claim that reward, however, the seeds of the retirement industry were planted. Some sociologists still claim that social security and its promise of retirement were nothing more than a new business venture our government created for itself. However it came about, the concept of retiring from the work force is now more common in America than in any other nation on earth, and the American retirement industry has become one of the fastest-growing forces in the economic landscape.

The pressure to prepare for retirement is enormous. Corporations tout their retirement plans when recruiting college graduates. The golden carrot offered to prospective employees is "good times later if you work hard now." Ironically, that "carrot" sometimes becomes a prod as early retirement is encouraged to accommodate corporate downsizing.

But for millions of people, retirement has become a myth.

The New Retirement

The American culture today is neatly divided into three classes of people: those who are gainfully employed, those who are unemployed, and those who are retired. Many in the second group have had their retirement dreams shattered by the loss of job or career. For them, dreams of shuffleboard and sunbathing on the sandy beaches in Florida have given way to the reality of economic survival. Those still employed question whether their resources will meet the costs of their retirement plans. Still others who have been retired are once again looking for work to meet rising prices. The social security system is becoming known as the social *insecurity* system in the face of receding funds.

This was brought home to me during a recent workshop when a well-groomed and very articulate gentleman shared his story as we stood together in the lunch line. He had worked for years in preparation for that happy time called retirement. Now in his early sixties, he was in the midst of a very expensive divorce and found his carefully guarded resources vanishing. He ended his story by telling me he was now employed thirty hours a week at a local fast-food restaurant. Forty-five years earlier, his first job as a teenager had been in a local diner in his hometown. To say he was somewhat bitter about being "right back where he started" would be an understatement. His situation is repeated annually in thousands of lives in the retirement area where I live—and across the nation.

In spite of these pained realities, the retirement dream remains alive for millions of people—just a few steps to the left of the rainbow of promise. Successful retirement will still depend largely on realistic expectations about money, time, health, and focused planning. Passive retirement, where many people in past generations merely waited to die, will be replaced by active retirement where second careers, entrepreneurship, and new challenges become the order of the day. In fact I believe the word *retirement* will take on new definitions as choices are expanded in the nineties; retirement may well come to mean "stopping something old and starting something new."

The Case against Retirement

One of the greatest struggles in retirement is coping with the loss of your identity. It seldom matters to anyone around you what you once were. What is important is what you are *now*. And the word *retired* just doesn't have the same ring as president of First National Bank.

This adjustment seems hardest for people like Joe, who retired from jobs of high-level authority and widespread responsibilities. A career military officer, Joe had been in the air force thirty years and was a colonel when he was passed over for the second time for promotion to general. It was time to go, and he tried to turn loose of his command gracefully.

He smiled through the "hail and farewell" celebration as his friends gathered for a gala send-off. He talked about plans to travel and "putter in the garden" and breed horses on his ranch in the Southwest. But when he pictured himself doing those things, his ego disintegrated. His high-level air force assignment had kept him shuttling between the Pentagon and various air bases throughout the country. Within that realm, he had worn a uniform that commanded instant respect. He didn't have to *tell* those around him he was a colonel. They could see the insignia he wore, and they responded with deference and courtesy.

All of that changed when he took the uniform off for the last time. I have listened to groups of retired people like Joe trying to impress each other with their former job titles—and it's soon obvious that those titles are about as important as yesterday's newspaper. The real plea of every retired person is to still be somebody.

Retirement communities are filled with once-important people who are living out their lives in personal obscurity. While most probably enjoy their new life of leisure, many others turn to drugs and alcohol, the silent killers in scores of retirement enclaves across America, to deaden the pain caused by loss of identity and self-worth. Prescription drugs follow close behind as the killer of past dreams and present realities. As a result, in many instances retirement kills people quicker than most diseases. It happens because it takes something from them that many are not ready to give up: their identity. Mundane card games and craft classes after a daily round of golf cannot give meaning and purpose to life after one has impacted others' lives for forty years.

In most cases, retired men lose their identities quicker and more often than retired women, perhaps because many women consider themselves still "employed" as homemakers, wives, and mothers. There are abundant tales of retired husbands following their wives around all day long, looking for some form of meaning and fulfillment. One lady I know recently told me she took a full-time job for the sole purpose of getting away from her retired husband, who followed her from room to room and mall to mall every day. She felt she had become his "new job." Another woman recently went back to school full-time to obtain a degree she really did not need in order to have space apart from the overpowering shadow of her retired husband. Many late-life divorces happen when the man cannot adjust to his new role and the wife gets pushed to the edge of retirement insanity.

I personally believe that no one should be forced to retire from the work he or she loves until it is impossible to go on due to ill health or some other extenuating circumstances. I am always amazed by the fact that people are expected to think about retirement from about age fifty-five on and make room in work forces for younger and supposedly brighter employees. Yet our country has often seemed to place great value in its state and national leaders being in the fifty-something category or older. Perhaps all the retired people should run for public office; those may be the only positions in America today where age doesn't matter! (And although Bill Clinton, born in 1946, and Al Gore, born in 1948, are considered young compared with more recent presidents and vice presidents, it's interesting to note that they, too, will be in or nearing the fifty-something years by the time their first term ends. Perhaps part of the nation's impression of them as young leaders comes from the new ideas they brought with them to their government posts.)

Early retirement may seem like the Great Escape if you hate your job or are unchallenged and bored by it. In that kind of situation you do not need early retirement but the opportunity for a new beginning. The disease of early retirement in America today is robbing scores of fifty-something people of their ability to make a difference in our world.

This occurs not only in lost productivity, but also in the way early retirement can be detrimental to our collective morale. The worst diseases are not the ones that rob us physically; the ones that rob our spirits are far more destructive. Simply being busy does not necessarily revive our spirits, but doing things with meaning attached to them does. In their book *What Men Are Like* John Sanford and George Lough say this revival of our spirits (they call it the "rounding out" of our "consciousness and personality") may be "what holds this shaky world of ours more or less together. When a person develops psychologically, he or she adds a small but vital increment of spiritual development and psychological wholeness to humanity. . . ."[1] What a pleasant thought: Just by being happy and doing something with meaning we can make the world a better place. This is the opposite of the unhappy retirees whose depression sends them into chronic illnesses that overwhelm medical facilities and drain the energy of the friends and relatives who try to care for them.

We constantly read stories of happy people who coasted through their first fifty years and really got their lives in high gear during their fifties and sixties. One example is comedian George Burns, born in 1896, who keeps inching closer to the one hundred mark. He has made no secret of the fact that he intends to do his comedy act in Las Vegas when he turns one hundred. In fact, it's been rumored that recently, at age ninety-seven, he signed a ten-year contract! His movie successes came well after his seventieth birthday. He continues to do what he has always done—only his pace has slowed. The famous writer James Michener, well into his eighties, continues to write best-sellers and do research for future books.

I will be fifty-nine this year. If someone filled my bank account with all the money I would ever need to meet my expenses, I would not quit writing, speaking, and counseling. What I do gives my life meaning, purpose, and identity. Without that, there would be no real life.

Retire and Expire, or Perspire with Desire

Around Thanksgiving each year, the annual migration of "snowbirds" arrives in Arizona, where I live. (Snowbirds are the thousands of retirees who leave the colder northern states each winter and head for the warmer temperatures throughout the South and Southwest.) The lines at restaurants become lengthy, and the traffic is frequently snarled with oversized motor homes trying to navigate through our streets. Mobile-home parks are filled along with condo developments, golf courses, and shopping malls.

I have watched this rite of winter for five years in Arizona and for the six years I lived in Florida. Churches go from one to three services on winter Sundays. An endless line of tour buses crawls through Phoenix day after winter day. The vast percentage of snowbirds are retirees who are looking for ways to fill their days and nights. Many will readily admit they are self-centered and more interested in taking than giving.

According to our local business analysts, the crowd is getting younger each year as many fifty-something people join the annual trek to warmer climes. Not a few are also armed with the want ads every winter in search of part-time or even full-time employment. As the average life span inches up to age seventy-four, we are increasingly facing people who will be retired for twenty to twenty-five years prior to death.

I raise several questions to all potential joiners of our local version of the retirement marathon (and to any who might head to other places):

1. Is there something more fulfilling you can do with your life in the next twenty years?
   _____ Yes   _____ No
   If yes, what?

   _____

   _____

2. Do you still possess gifts in your life that others need to receive? _____ Yes   _____ No

If yes, what?

_____

_____

3. Do you really need to indulge yourself for the next twenty years? _____ Yes _____ No
   If yes, why?

_____

_____

4. Is living in a closed community with other retirees healthy for you mentally, emotionally, physically, and spiritually?
   _____ Yes _____ No
   If yes, why?

_____

_____

5. Are there still some goals to accomplish in your life?
   _____ Yes _____ No
   If yes, what are they?

_____

_____

6. Will anyone be able to pick you out of the crowd of retirees after five years? _____ Yes _____ No
   If yes, why?

_____

_____

7. Did you retire just to join the line of those waiting to expire? _____ Yes _____ No
   If yes, why?

   _____

   _____

8. Do you have at least one or more persons who really need you? _____ Yes _____ No
   If yes, who?

   _____

   _____

No matter where we are in life, we need to make the wisest use of our gifts, talents, and abilities. In retirement we can choose indulgence or we can choose investment. Indulgence says, *I have worked hard and long and now I can do what I want.* Investment says, *There are others who need what I can give, so I will continue to give.* Mother Teresa, founder of the Sisters of Charity, is in her early eighties and recently stated she could never retire even if her health were declining because the needs around her are still so great. The poor of the world can never retire, and for her to retire from them would be self-indulgent.

The concept of "retire and then expire" needs to be replaced with the challenge of "desire and perspire." A rewarding retirement is not one that fills your time with an incessant agenda of purposeless pursuits. Filling time is easy. Investing time is more difficult because you work for a return. An investment demands energy, talent, and creativity along with the desire to make a difference through hard work. Many retirees may find that they are running *from* something rather than *toward* something that can be meaningful and fulfilling.

The Challenge of Creative Retirement

For those who do not need financial remuneration, creative retirement is a way to continue serving others while adding meaning to your own life. This is being done in small ways by millions of people through volunteer programs in hospitals, the Red Cross, rehabilitation centers, and thousands of similar programs in every city across America. Without volunteers, many effective care programs would not exist. Yet volunteers represent only a fraction of the retirement population today. Many who volunteer in their retirement years are simply continuing to do what they have done throughout their lives. Their joy is simply in giving of themselves to others.

A few years ago in my home church, the bulletin announced that a couple was to be commissioned for a year of missionary service overseas. I expected a young couple to step forward. I was thoroughly surprised when a gray-haired couple, older than I, came down the aisle. Both were newly retired schoolteachers and for years they had looked forward to this opportunity to invest their gifts, talents, and abilities on a foreign mission field. How many other couples and singles could accept a similar challenge? How many former medical personnel could invest a few retirement years to fill much-needed gaps in hospitals around the world? There is no limit to the challenges of creatively using segments of your retirement years in service opportunities. One good missions trip before retirement will readily convince you of the need.

Creative retirement is also an opportunity to receive further education in areas you have long wanted to explore. I will never forget the retired schoolteacher who announced that her future goal was to obtain her doctorate degree. She told me she always wanted a doctorate and now finally had time to get one. Most people would think that to be a waste of time and money, but it isn't to someone who values growth.

If there is no need to continue to earn an income, retirement can be a newfound freedom to pursue personal growth. We need to have more respect for the work of learning more about ourselves, learning to get in touch with inner feelings, thoughts, needs, and dreams. In most people's working life, there is little time for developing the inner man or woman. The urgent is pursued while the inner is denied. It is never too late to discover who we are on the inside.

Creative retirement may mean living a new lifestyle in a different country, state, or city. Learning a new language along with local customs can challenge the safe comfort zone in all of us. Experiencing a different history from your own can give you a global understanding that Sun City, Arizona, could never quite match. Seeing the needs of others can bring a new sense of thankfulness into your own life and cause you to live a less self-centered existence.

Creative retirement may also mean that you start something new. One of the best examples was Colonel Harland Sanders of Kentucky Fried Chicken fame, who was in his sixties when he launched his world-famous chain. He is just one of millions of fifty-something (and older) Americans who have used their "retirement years" to launch themselves into new adventures of productive living. In the past ten years alone, the number of self-employed Americans fifty-five or older has increased dramatically, and there are now more than two million fifty-something entrepreneurs who have started their own private businesses.

If you're not up to starting a new business, consider trying a new career—or a collection of several careers simultaneously. Writing for *Modern Maturity,* Charles Handy notes that many people accept early retirement, hoping to receive a pension while working at a similar job with a different company. He suggests that "a better solution [than another full-time job] . . . would be bits and pieces of work for different organizations, clients, or communities; work for customers, not employees."

Handy also suggests a change in attitude and name for this period of our lives, calling it "the third age of living" instead of "retirement." With this attitude, he says, "eventually, we shall all recognize that a full-time job is only one part of the journey and that we must prepare ourselves better for our Third Age of Living. Eventually, we shall all realize that the answer to job and/or marriage burnout is not less of the same or more of some antidote, but change—change, before it is too late, to a 'portfolio' way of thinking."[2]

In its June 4, 1990 issue, *U.S. News and World Report* suggested several possibilities for this creative-retirement option in an article titled, "Hitting the unretirement circuit: Older Americans have more job opportunities than they think." Writer Marc Silver noted that banks, hotels, travel agencies, hardware stores, and temporary agencies are "clamoring for mature workers" who are willing to work part-time. As examples Silver cited Bank of America, Days Inn, Builders Emporium, Home Depot, Hechinger, and temporary agencies including Kelly, Adia, and Volt.

Eventually Joe, the air force retiree mentioned earlier, developed a portfolio of "retirement careers." In frustration after almost a year of unsuccessfully finding another full-time job, he accepted a part-time position to teach a basic business course at the local branch of the state technical college, "just to have something to do." The contacts he made with the technical college's administration led to his being appointed by the governor to the state board looking into ways to overhaul the technical-college system. And when his proposal to that board received favorable press coverage, he was offered a lucrative consulting contract. Soon he found his work week filled once more, but with a variety of assignments. He still taught the business class two days a week at the technical college, but now he was also meeting with the state board and fulfilling consulting assignments.

When the Money Won't Support the Dream

This "portfolio" approach does have its down side, however, for fifty-something people who are forced into part-time work unwillingly, especially if they have no pension or other backup income. Part-time work usually offers no health care, insurance, or retirement benefits (one of the cost-saving reasons many corporations are phasing out older full-time workers in favor of part-time employees). And the sad truth is that these benefits are more needed for older employees than younger ones.

The potential extent of this problem is becoming frightening as the work force in America continues to eject fifty-something people from its ranks. In the many surveys we received from fifty-something people, about 75 percent of them expressed concern that they had no solid retirement plan outside of social security. Many stated they never had extra money to save for a "rainy day" because every day in their lives had seemed like a rainy day! As they viewed the years ahead, many slowly realized they would never have the money to support their traditional retirement dream.

All this adds up to the sad fact that the nineties may be the first decade to bury the brass ring at the end of a career. The traditional retirement of full-time leisure becomes a myth for all except the wealthy. The other 80 percent of us will need to become resourceful, creative, and adventuresome in the last decades of our lives. But that's not so bad. I believe we will have a physically and mentally healthier older population as a result of those challenges.

Self-employed people may be the best equipped mentally and emotionally to face the retirement myth because they have learned to be responsible for their own destinies, and they have learned to trust their own gifts, talents, abilities, and creative options. They are not bound by the controlling factors of giant companies and can often draw upon unlimited resources when called to face frightening situations. The entrepreneurial spirit is a spirit of survival and challenge.

Continuing Your Career

Many fifty-something people have yet another option —the one that everyone used to think was a way of life: continuing on in the career of your choice. If you love what you do and it gives meaning and purpose to your life, you should be able to do it as long as you choose. One way to make that happen, if your company doesn't enforce a mandatory retirement age, is to consciously work to maintain yourself as a productive, efficient part of your employer's team.

Researchers Chrystie Meziere and Robert Hansson offer these additional strategies for prolonging your work life:

- Broaden your career options. Pursue on-the-job training.
- Maintain a positive self-presentation. Be careful about your personal appearance.
- Reduce the risks in health and job security. . . . Maintain a healthy diet. Avoid job-related health hazards.
- Continue professional and personal development.
- Manage your workload and resources. Reduce your job stress by distributing your work load across time and other people.[3]

Having the energy to remain actively employed during your fifty-something years may mean you take longer lunch breaks and go to bed before the late news, but if you have a satisfying job to go to every morning your happiness level will remain high and you will never wonder how to fill the days of your week.

Edging toward the Future

We all face unexpected and unplanned-for events as we journey through life, and even our best-laid plans for the future can go awry. Pension plans can evaporate when investment firms fail, banks and savings and loans can close, companies can be sold to foreign investors, and employees with tenure can be ushered out the door to a forbidding and uncertain future. The social security system may finally go under as some predict. If we could control everything, we would keep our ducks in a row every day of our lives. We can't. There are no guarantees anymore. The sooner we understand that and begin to make course corrections, the less fearful we will be about our future.

The faith-based person knows God holds all tomorrows in His hand. God understands life's confusions and contradictions, and He guarantees that He will watch over us. It is the only real guarantee we are left with in life, but it is the best one!

This chapter has raised some scary issues. Forced retirement, purposeless retirement, loss of identity and meaning, financial decline, and changing lifestyles will impact all of us in various ways as we look to the future. Some of us will still feel very secure while others will be fearful and insecure. If we already have good plans for our future, we need to review and update them and consider alternatives in case those plans become unworkable. If we just live from day to day and have no plans, it is time to make some.

Take a time-out to complete the sentences below. Use your responses to consider how you will make the most of your retirement years—whether or not you actually retire.

1. When I retire, I plan to:

_____

_____

_____

2. If my retirement plans fall apart, I will:

_____

_____

_____

3. I don't ever plan to retire because:

_____

_____

_____

4. My greatest fear about retirement is:

_____

_____

_____

5. The thing that has caught my attention the most in this chapter is:

_____

_____

_____

6. The things I really need to work on are:

_____

_____

_____

7. A great second career for me would be:

_____

_____

_____

10

Children Are Forever

As my father planted for me, so do I plant for my children.

The Talmud

RECENTLY I BECAME a victim of the child-rearing myth! What is that myth all about? It centers on the belief that all parents have to do is push or pull their children through high school graduation, then the children will move out of the house, take aim at college or career, and nevermore return except for happy visits. Along with the reward of an empty room or two this myth brings the hope that said children will assume responsibility for their economic survival the minute they move out from under the parents' roof.

Millions of parents have fallen for this myth. Did it happen to you too?

While many children do follow the plan and live up to parental dreams, a large group of them begin a career of moving in and out of their parents' house—each time with the continued promise that the current move in or out will be the last. Still others never even pack a box or move toward the door. Two, four, six years after high school graduation, they may still be settled in their old bedroom, eating your food, wearing out your house, and complaining when their laundry isn't done.

With the economic realities facing today's older children, it is little wonder that sometimes the only event that will dislodge them from your home is their marriage. And even that doesn't always work; instead, you gain another resident!

My wife and I lived through several years of having our children move in and move out. I think we finally solved our problem by moving away and leaving no forwarding address! Finally, relief was spelled "empty house."

Fast-forward a few years and two of our three children are married now with children of their own. They have their own residences, families, and lives. Now we find ourselves wondering what they are doing, why they don't call, when they will visit, and if they are all right. The myth has been buried, but the need for connectedness grows stronger with each passing day. We are more fortunate than most parents because we are only an hour away by plane and six hours away by car; it's a sometimes-comfortable distance.

Viewing Your Children through the Lens of Mortality

I think I have finally learned the truth. *Children are forever, and being a parent is a lifetime sentence.* You will need them, and they will continue to need you. You'll see that for yourself as the years go by and your phone bills go up.

The fifty-something years are a time of viewing family and children through a different lens. In your thirties and forties, you probably felt you would be around each other forever. If the fifty-something years offer the first glimpse of mortality, they also help you understand for the first time that you will not always be present for your children, and the day will come when they will no longer share their lives with you.

I remember when I first started thinking about all this a few years ago. I had a hard time accepting the reality that someday I would only be present to them in memory and photograph. I have a hard time dealing with that even as I write these words. It is far more of a reality for me than it is for them. They expect me to live forever just as I expected my parents to live forever. When I try to talk with them about this, they change the topic quickly. To them, Mom and Dad are still immortal.

When my parents died, I was left to keep living the best way I could. They had given little thought of how to equip me to live without them, and I had given little thought to it, myself.

The Gifts We Leave Behind

One of the greatest concerns I think about in my late fifties is what I will leave behind as gifts to my children. Not the material gifts but the motivational, spiritual, emotional, and inspirational *inner gifts* I can give them as a living legacy. I will be more remembered by those gifts than by anything tangible.

One of the advantages of thinking about this in the fifty-something years is that there is still time to do some homework in this gift-giving area. Most of us are so consumed with living in our first fifty years that we spend little time trying to share our inner beings with our children. Most communication is of the maintenance variety. We talk little about what we believe and why, what motivates and inspires us, and how we feel emotionally.

I have a strong feeling that the older our children become, the less meaningful communication we have with them. As young adults with families of their own they are just as consumed as we were when they were our little children. As parents and grandparents, we float in and out of their lives with random visits and telephone updates. We don't even take the time to tell them how we feel about growing older and what our fears might be. We believe they have enough to deal with in their own families. And there's something else that holds us back. Self-revelation always has its risks that we may be misunderstood and considered to be on the edge of being maudlin. But in allowing our deep feelings and concerns to go unspoken, we rob our children of the model our inner strength could be as a resource for *their* inner strength.

What Do Your Children Need from You? What Do You Need from Them?

When our children were young, we needed them to need us and to give and receive love. There was nothing complex about that relationship. Hugs and outstretched arms were the signposts, laughter and tears the thermometer. Issues were as simple as taking a bath and turning out the lights and as profound as why good grades were important and why the stars did not fall from the sky.

As the children grew older, they formed their own identities and began to move away from us toward their maturity. Relieved, we began to realize they soon would be on their own and we would have some breathing room at long last.

When the last child leaves home, most parents experience an "intermission" as they examine their scar tissue from child-rearing, tell all their horror stories, and vow they would never go through that again. Happiness and sadness commingle with the reality that the children are finally on their own. (*We hope!*)

The intermission concludes when the children marry and start having their own children. I don't think most parents take their children seriously as adults until the children begin having children. Suddenly, you realize they have the heavy responsibilities that you once had, and your overall concern for everything about them intensifies. It is easy to forget that they are probably no more ready for parenting than you were a few decades ago.

But this can be a factor that draws you closer as you share your experiences from the past and marvel at how child-rearing techniques have changed or remained the same. Alice Rossi, a fellow at the John D. and Catherine T. MacArthur Foundation's Research Network on Successful Midlife Development, notes that "intimacy with children, which bottoms out from ages fifteen to nineteen, climbs steeply through the [children's] twenties and thirties. One of the things to look forward to in midlife is the continuity and shared interests that will come as your children in turn become parents."[1]

Another process occurs when the grandchildren are born: The children's quest for parental approval starts all over again. Then we discover very quickly that our children need to have us love them all over again by loving their children. They also need to know that we will still be there for them when they need us.

And what do we need from them? Confirmation that we were good parents and are still worthy of their love. And bragging rights that they will be kind and loving parents because we were kind and loving parents. This could be linked to what Carol Ryff, associate director of the Institute on Aging and Adult Life at the University of Wisconsin at Madison, says is one of the "underestimated family pleasures . . . the satisfaction that parents take in knowing that grown-up children have turned out all right."[2]

We also need our adult children to be physically present in our lives, perhaps more than they need us to be close by. They and their families are the validation for our existence. Their joys and sorrows in building their families will be ours as well. We will celebrate and we will commiserate with them, and life will go on.

Several issues affect your relationship with your adult children during your fifty-something years. In the rest of this chapter we'll look at the most common ones.

Spirituality

What do you do when your children's lifestyle is a world apart from yours? The answer seems easy: You let them do their thing and you do yours. But that's easier said than done! If you brought up your children in a religious environment where they were taught principles and standards from the Bible, you expect, hope, and pray that they will do the same for their children. Many times that does not happen, and your children and grandchildren grow up without that special influence that was important to you.

It is tough to sit on the curb in your fifties and watch your children pass through life without the spiritual guidance that is such an essential part of your own existence. You wonder what you can do to spark in them the same zest you feel in God's presence. Sure, you can nudge them gently and pray sincerely that they will come to share your vision. But our adult children must make their own choices—and live with the consequences. Watching our loved ones live out that fact is a burden many fifty-something parents carry every day. Like them, I carry it too.

The Geography Question

There have been moments in my life when I would have liked to have the family living arrangements of the Ewings on the TV show "Dallas." The mother, adult children, and their families all lived together in the big house at Southfork. In happy moments (and admittedly those are few and far between on a soap opera!) it looked like a lot of fun and closeness. But in times of conflict, it looked too close.

Unless a job makes the decision for you, the geography question has to be faced sometime. How do you decide whether to live close to your children or far away? Is it important to live close by? How did you feel about living close to your parents thirty years ago? If your family was a closely knit brood as your children grew up, there will be a greater need for ongoing closeness than if you were simply a group sharing equal living space. Some family members have strong, independent spirits and do not feel the need to be geographically or emotionally close to each other.

Before a decision is made, family members need to talk about how important it really is for them to be close to each other. Ethnic families in our culture often have a very strong sense of family bonding; it is commonplace for them to live in seven or eight houses within a few blocks of each other. The children grow up knowing a host of aunts, uncles, nephews, and nieces as well as grandparents. Special events are shared by all, and there is a strong sense of the importance of the family and all its members.

As we fifty-something parents age, most of us find it comforting to have our children nearby and know that they can give us help when needed. It is also important to have our grandchildren close by, something we'll discuss in the next chapter. But too much closeness can smother growth just as too much distance can isolate. The secret is found in a happy balance.

Sharing the Joy

This past Fourth of July, my wife and I were in Prescott, Arizona, to conduct a retreat. In the afternoon we went down to the courthouse square and found, on the grassy lawn surrounding the courthouse, families picnicking, children playing, and various booths peddling arts and crafts. Live music went on all afternoon. We agreed it was a great place to bring a family for the Fourth.

But our children and their families were four hundred miles away in California, and that made us feel very alone. We were making a memory; we just did not have the opportunity to share it with our family.

If living life is the making of memories, some of our best memories should be found in times of family celebration. Sometimes it takes a determined effort to get everyone together for holiday gatherings. Compromises are needed, and schedules sometimes have to be rearranged. If the parents and children are scattered, it's often easier for the grandparents to go to the children's homes than it is for the children to pack up all their babies' traveling paraphernalia and come to the grandparents' house. This is especially true if the grandparents are retired and have more leisure time for traveling than do their job-limited children.

When to Help and When Not to Help

In midlife, parents' relationship with their adult children can take on a whole new meaning. Often the parents are looked upon as affluent while the children feel poverty-stricken and devoid of all the wonderful things their parents possess. Parents are easily caught in the trap of wanting the best for their children and grandchildren, and often they find themselves supplying needed loans or gifts for a vast assortment of acquisitions.

Babysitting

Grandparents often make perfect babysitters; they have a loving interest in their grandchildren and thus want to make sure they're well cared for. In addition, babysitting lets them spend one-on-one time with the little ones who mean so much to them. But there are drawbacks to the babysitting issue, too, as many grandparents can confirm.

"We love our granddaughter, and we enjoy spending time with her," said one fifty-something grandmother. "But my son and his wife began asking us to watch her when she was about a month old, and over the next two years it became more and more frequent until my husband and I realized it had been more than a year since we had made any special weekend plans just to do what *we* wanted to do. We found ourselves staying home and watching TV more than we had or turning down friends who asked us to do something with them because we always felt we had to be 'on call' in case the kids wanted us to watch Jessica. Our house started looking like a nursery; we had riding toys in the living room and a playpen in the kitchen. And the problem wasn't that we resented this new turn our life had taken; we didn't. But we were focusing on the grandbaby; she took precedence over everything else, even our own relationship."

It finally occurred to these grandparents that they would be better grandparents, especially as Jessica got older, if they had "a life of our own," as the grandmother said. "We made it a point to start doing things again just for ourselves—things that we enjoyed. We went to the Gulf Coast with another couple. We started volunteering with Meals on Wheels. We even joined a local theater group. And as Jessica got older, she loved hearing about the things we did; sometimes she came with us. And as a result, I think we're all a lot happier and we enjoy being with each other more."

Financial Help

One of the longest-playing family disputes in the lives of fifty-something parents is whether to help their children financially. It is a decision that is almost always shrouded by guilt that says, "We have so much and they have so little," or "If we don't help our children, who will?" or "In today's economy, they will never have anything if we don't help them."

After fighting some of these battles personally with our children, I am convinced that giving children financial help is generally more guilt-based than love-based. It is sometimes more difficult to do the loving thing than the guilt-directed thing. When love says no, we sometimes have to live with children who think we are hard-hearted. When guilt says yes, we become the heroes of those seeking our help. It is definitely more fun to be a hero!

Advice

If the struggle to decide whether to help our children with money is first, it is followed closely by the sometimes overwhelming urge to offer advice, input, directions, and guidance. I have discovered that my children seek my expertise far less than I have the desire to give it! Like most fifty-something parents, I have something wise to say about everything on planet earth. After all, I have spent many years collecting all this wisdom! However, the sad truth is that my children (and all other earthly inhabitants) are not very interested.

As we watch our children struggle with life and its issues, we desperately want to tell them we struggled with the same things and allow them to profit from our wisdom and avoid our mistakes. It is especially hard to stay detached and uninvolved when children are experiencing marital conflicts, personality clashes, discipline differences, and career struggles. To keep our space and give them theirs becomes a constant challenge. The counselor-caregiver part of me wants to jump in and give advice and direction and make my children's problems disappear. The funny thing is that no one did that for me, and I learned by my experiences. I just hate to see someone else collect the necessary scar tissue to validate the process.

When Families Come Apart

Another area where parents want to help comes when divorce shatters the marriage of a son or daughter. Immediately, parents feel they have failed somehow when their children go through a divorce. The parents' own guilt, fear, anger, and sense of failure can project them into the middle of the conflict with their guns blazing in defense of their child. Or it can send them into hiding and denial.

Divorce disrupts and divides entire family systems because it compels people to choose whom they want to support. Mothers and fathers, sisters and brothers often end up on opposite sides of the wall built by divorce. For years I have advised family members not to take sides in a divorce experience, but the financial logistics of a divorce seldom make this advice workable.

Increasingly I have watched children and grandchildren move in with parents after a divorce, seeking the stability and nourishment a primary home can provide for hurting people when their own home falls apart. The real struggle for everyone in these situations is to deal with this interruption to both of their family units. Living adjustments do not come easily for most people. Good intentions can end up spawning resentments that leave greater scars than the divorce experience.

When Jobs Are Lost

One day your children can be doing well in their careers and keeping up with their bills. The next day they can be unemployed with bill collectors at their door. Homes can be foreclosed, autos repossessed, and bankruptcy can become a looming reality. Overnight, your son or daughter's family can be sitting on the curb with no place to go.

It is hard for a parent to know what to do in this ever-increasing reality in today's world. Those of us who are older lived in a more stable economy during most of our lifetimes. Economic downturns were merely small potholes in our journey; recovery always reappeared. Today, this is no longer true. It is difficult enough when we fifty-something people are standing in unemployment lines; it is absolutely gut-wrenching when a member of our family is standing in line behind us.

Even those who have a comfortable fifty-something lifestyle may not have the ability to provide "care insurance" for their children. Today few fifty-something people have endless resources to pump into their children's bank accounts. In fact, some parents end up looking to their children for economic help when their children may be only one step away from looking to their parents.

The Gift That Matters Most

It takes an infinite amount of wisdom, guidance, and prayer to know when to jump in to each other's problems and when to remain on the sidelines. Pride can keep both sides from asking for help when it is needed, and fear of meddling can prevent it from being offered. The catalyst that finally makes things happen, one way or the other, is love.

Death, disease, divorce, dysfunctions—all these problems and more tend to send children in search of help from their parents. They come to us, hoping we can somehow ease their pain and help them through the crisis. This response has always been accepted by those who know that parenting is a lifetime calling. Real families are not just people who go their own way and do their own thing without sharing either success or failure. Real families are people who are connected forever through the bonds of love and care.

No matter what else we do for our children, this is the

thing that matters most: that we constantly love them. When we must decline to take specific actions—give them money, watch their children, intervene on their behalf—we do so lovingly, believing this is the best decision for them and for our relationship with them.

How Do You Handle Parenting Issues?

Think about the parenting issues we've discussed here —babysitting, giving advice, helping adult children cope with divorce or job loss—and review how you handle them by filling out the chart below.

A Time-Out to Review My Fifty-Something Parenting Skills

When my children ask for or need . . .	I usually (or I think I might) . . .	It would be better if I . . .
Money	Loan it to them and then get upset when they don't pay me back	Just gave it to them and said NO more often.
Advice	Give it to them and complain because they don't follow it.	Suggest they ask someone else.
Friendship	Am too busy.	
Babysitting	_____	_____
Help because of a divorce	_____	_____

Help because of a
job loss   _____   _____

Help because of
death or illness   _____   _____

_____   _____   _____

_____   _____   _____

_____   _____   _____

_____   _____   _____

_____   _____   _____

_____   _____   _____

_____   _____   _____

_____   _____   _____

_____   _____   _____

_____   _____   _____

_____   _____   _____

_____   _____   _____

_____   _____   _____

_____   _____   _____

Take some time to fill out this "time-out" as it relates to you.

And the Winner Is . . .

Every family system has its own unique form and identity, with each new branch taking off in a different direction. If a primary family has six different branches some will bear little resemblance to the primary unit. After a few generations, the progeny can look more like a foreign legion than the family of origin.

Some families follow the same track for a hundred years or more; tradition, honor, and respect keep all the various generations heading in the same direction. Staying within geographical boundaries helps maintain this kind of continuity. Those of us who are the scattered remnants and lonely pilgrims of our primary family often wish we were the Smiths of Boston or the Whites of Delaware, with our clan converging every summer for a month at the historic family compound at Cape Cod. The reality is that most of us are nomads from everywhere with no family compound anywhere. We are the changing face of the family in America.

Perhaps the best we can do in our fifty-something years is sound the wake-up call to our family members and deepen our relationships with them. Fifty-something can be a time when your family floats away from you with no imminent return in sight, or it can be a time of making a concerted effort at pulling your loved ones together and redefining what *family* really is.

11

Happiness Is Being a Fifty-Something Grandparent

I want to be a supplementary emotional vitamin, to be taken often enough to make the realities of the everyday world more endurable for my grandchild!

Eda LeShan

I BECAME A grandparent for the first time in my early fifties. I was conducting a seminar in Ohio when the good news came across the telephone lines. Twenty-four hours later, I held my grandson in my arms and desperately wished he was old enough to play baseball with me or at least say hello. Unlike the many people who warned me that I would feel very old when I became a grandparent, I felt younger than ever and could not wait to involve myself in the growing-up experiences of this child named Ryan.

As Ryan and I, along with my other three grandchildren, Kelsey, Kendall, and Kory, have grown together, I have found myself reflecting more and more on my own grandparents and what they so profoundly contributed to my early years. My grandfather was the school custodian at my elementary school and we lived in the country only a few miles apart, so he was in my life every day as a trusted friend and a listening ear. I could hop on my bicycle anytime I wanted and go to his house. My grandmother baked anything and everything she knew I would eat. Grandfather told me endless stories about his life growing up in England and fighting in World War I. We listened to hockey games and prizefighting on the radio together. (My hockey memories from those days are so strong today that I recently ordered a Toronto Maple Leafs hockey shirt to wear when my nostalgia overtakes me.) He was always sending me to the store to buy his pipe tobacco and cigars, and he made sure there was always extra money for soda or ice cream for me.

I remember his gold pocket watch, his war medals, his walking stick, and the smell of his shaving lotion. He always had a beagle hound or two that we hunted rabbits with in the winter. We planted gardens of flowers and vegetables every spring and painted his house a different color every summer. Grandmother sewed and cooked and let me sleep on her feather bed. Until I went to high school, I probably spent more time with my grandparents than I did with my parents. They were loving, caring, and easy to be around. They taught me things and made me feel I belonged to them in a deep and personal way. Early in my life, I became a believer in the importance of grandparents.

The Grandparent Gap

Grandparenting has changed dramatically over the past fifty years. Families that once lived close to each other are now separated by thousands of miles and differing lifestyles.

As America ages, the grandparent population will increase dramatically. In our surveys it was common for many respondents in their early fifties to have several grandchildren, with more on the way. One respondent at age fifty-four had eight grandchildren!

This era of grandparents is also a rising economic force when you realize that grandparent households spend an average of $819 annually on their grandchildren. Living close or distant from grandchildren has little impact on this spending.

Jeff Ostroff, author of *Successful Marketing to the 50+ Consumer,* said, "The most significant growth segment of the population will be older Americans. From 1990 to 2000, the number of Americans older than 45 will increase by 8.5 million." As a result of the tremendous growth in this age group, marketing and research firms are targeting older audiences, and the media are giving more attention to those over age fifty.

Grandparents like I had are more of a rarity today. Many of the children I meet barely even know their grandparents; their only connection is by family pictures and birthday cards. The camaraderie, closeness, and care that only a grandparent can give will never impact their lives. The wisdom of years of living that grandparents possess will never be shared—and the grandchildren will be the losers. (In contrast, another current phenomenon is grandparents who are solely responsible for their grandchildren, an issue we'll look at a little later in this chapter.)

The prime time for intimacy and involvement between grandparents and grandchildren is from birth to about age twelve or thirteen. As children age, they move more into their own world of peer pressure and peer support.

Very few teenagers would be caught shopping at the mall with their grandparents or even going fishing with them. However, active grandparents almost always become favorite playmates for young children. There is no stigma for this under-twelve group about being around wrinkles and gray hair; in fact, grandparents are something to brag about to one's under-twelve friends. *Grandparents are awesome to little children.* They usually have more money, more time, more power, more wisdom, and more humor than any child's father or mother. And best of all, they can be bribed! I heard a real zinger the other day: "Do you know why grandparents and grandchildren love each other and get along with each other so well? It's because they have a mutual enemy (the parents)!"

Healthy relationships between grandparents and grandchildren are often in direct proportion to the relationship the children's parents have with their parents. If the parents are close to their own children, the chances are far greater that the grandchildren will also be close to their grandparents. Parents are responsible for encouraging and supporting healthy grandparent structures for their children.

Many families live in a constant state of crisis and conflict, making effective grandparenting an impossibility. Grandparents often try to offset problems in families by sitting on the sidelines and "monitoring" what is going on, ready to jump in and help if needed, but hoping that won't be necessary.

The Gift of Grandparents

It is a special gift to children when they know they can visit grandparents who live in a distant city or state, perhaps spending a few weeks every summer. The expectations, regimentation, and discipline that children live with all year long can take a backseat to a few weeks of freedom and celebration at one's grandparents. It can be a time when children thrive in an environment of the grandparents' unconditional love. It can also give the grandparents a level of enjoyment that they perhaps never had when their own children were that age.

Redesigned Grandparents

Today, grandparents do not look like they did in those old family albums of years gone by: the stoic grandfather standing in suit and beard beside the portly grandmother seated in the wing chair. Today's grandfather may drive a sporty convertible and wear the same kind of clothes an older grandchild is wearing. He may be an avid sportsman and work out at a gym three times a week. Grandmother may run around town in a sweatsuit, take aerobics classes at the YWCA, have a part-time job, and be working on a degree at the local college. Grandparents may hike the mountains or ride the river rapids on the weekend. How they look and what they do with their time sends a loud message, "I may be a grandparent but I'm definitely not old!"

Up Close or at a Distance?

The thought of living at the other end of the country from my grandchildren is not even an option for me. I wonder how any grandparents who really love their grandchildren can only see them once or twice a year. I know that we can't all have the ideal arrangement of having our grandkids close by, but someplace in our land of disintegrating family structures and values, family closeness deserves a second look.

I have listened to many grandparents tell me it was time to do their own thing, and they wanted no family shackles around them. These remote grandparents feel they have earned their freedom, and they want to pursue it sans family members. Perhaps they are the tired among us who used up all their energy and interest in raising their own children. Now the thought of having to give anything more to grandchildren sends them motor-homing across America and hiding out in little-known campgrounds.

Many fifty-something grandparents head for one of the many retirement communities scattered throughout the country, especially across the South. Many of these places promote their facilities for "young-active" retirees and bill themselves as "child-free zones." Many pre- and post-retirement communities have a firm rule that its residents must be totally unencumbered by children residing with them. Children under age eighteen are granted certain limited visitation rights, but if they stay too long, one has a feeling the "child patrol" will ferret them out, transport them outside the gate entrance, and fine the violators.

It may not be long before the sign with a child painted on it and a slash mark through it is placed at the entrance of many of these communities. There are probing questions in all of this:

1. Do we stay younger with children around or with them absent?
2. Is a child-free zone a form of self-indulgence that eventually prohibits nourishing relationships?

3. Does this form of isolation contribute to the further decline in family systems in our culture?

Even if you choose to (or have no choice and must) live a distant and separate existence from your grandchildren, there are still some things you can do to keep a live, caring tie with them. Take the Grandparenting Test to see how your grandparenting measures up.

The Grandparenting Test

Do you do this?

	Yes	No

1. Call your grandchildren weekly and talk with them about what they are doing in their world. Show interest in their lives and allow them to show interest in yours. Tell them you miss them and that you love them. Consistent communication is vital to any growing relationship.   _____   _____

2. Make sure they exchange snapshots and family videos with you. To see each other is to send the message, "I'm still around and I care about you." Family events can be shared through home videos even when the family cannot all be present. Living life is the making of a memory, and memories are always best when shared.   _____   _____

3. Write letters and send little things that say "I love you" through the mail. Significant dates, like birthdays and holidays, are as important in the life of a child as they are in the

lives of adults. Special accomplishments also need special recognition from grandparents. _____ _____

4. Record stories on audio or video tapes and send them along to your grandkids. They can be replayed hundreds of times—and will be. _____ _____

5. If you are a grandparent living miles away from grandchildren, plan to have them visit you as often as you visit them. As they get older, you can have them meet you for a few days at Disneyland or some other exciting place. One of my best memories with my grandfather was going with him alone to the Canadian National Exhibition every summer. _____ _____

6. Display the things your grandchildren make at home or school around your home. Send things to your grandchildren that they can display to remind them of you. Our rooms and homes should contain the things that remind us of our human connectedness, the fact that I am not just me and you are not just you. We are a composite, a mosaic of many things and we need to frame our lives within that mosaic. My grandson loves to look at the pictures in my study of his mother as a young child, teenager, and young adult. _____ _____

What are grandparents for? Eda LeShan, in *The Wonderful Crisis of Middle Age,* said,

I think grandparents are for spoiling children; this has always been to some degree, and ought only to become more so, their chief role. The demands, the expectations, the conditions we set for young children are an unrelieved and awful burden—somewhere, somehow, there ought to be emotional relief from all the frustrations and restrictions our children live with. Grandparents are the perfect choice. They ought to let their grandchildren stay up later, eat more junk food, bounce on the furniture and get toys they don't need. What the grandchildren need is someone who loves them crazily, blindly and without reservation.

Maybe this really means that parents are charged with building character in their children, while grandparents can enjoy just being characters with their grandchildren!

In research and conversations with people regarding this question—what are grandparents for?—I have come up with a list for grandparent usage:

1. Grandparents are for giving and receiving unconditional love in big doses.
2. Grandparents are for mentoring because they often have far more patience—plus more experience—than parents.
3. Grandparents are for wiping away tears that are the direct result of life's most wounding and hurting experiences. Divorce is one of the largest.
4. Grandparents are for corny jokes, too many sweets, toys that make no sense, and clothes they think the grandchild will look good in but may be too large or too small.

5. Grandparents are for telling stories over and over about how things were when they were that age.
6. Grandparents are for BB guns, yo-yos, harmonicas, pocket knives, and other frightening or frivolous toys parents won't buy. They all precede Nintendo.
7. Grandparents are for long walks down country roads and catching butterflies.
8. Grandparents are for reading books to you when only the pictures make sense.
9. Grandparents are people who let you stay up late and fall asleep in their lap.
10. As one little boy said, grandparents are "people who always take your hand when you are out in public because they forget that you are not three now."

Changing Roles

Grandparent roles are continuing to change as we move through the nineties. With scary economic forecasts leading our newscasts nightly, another role change may soon overtake the grandparent world: Grandparents who are gainfully employed in their fifties may be looking at being just as gainfully employed in their sixties and seventies. This could change grandparenting roles in regard to available time and energy as well as disposable income. Our Norman Rockwell picture of Grandpa rocking on the porch smoking his pipe while Grandma makes fudge for the grandchildren may be replaced by Grandpa working two jobs and Grandma clipping money-saving coupons from the daily paper before she goes to her temporary job.

Currently the three most prominent changes in grandparents' roles are: the grandparent as substitute parent, the grandparent with legal rights to children after the death or divorce of a parent, and the grandparent as daycare provider.

Grandparents as Parents or Guardians

In July 1992, the Senate Special Committee on Aging announced that the number of children with grandparents as primary caregivers has increased 40 percent in the past decade. They further stated that 3.2 million children are now being cared for by their grandparents, and the increasing trend is due largely to growing numbers of out-of-wedlock births and a rise in drug abuse, alcohol abuse, and violent crime involving parents.

Several weeks ago, I watched a television talk show where the guests were all grandparents who had sole or partial custody of their grandchildren and were raising them in place of their parents. Some of the grandparents were angry and bitter that they had been left with this responsibility while others seemed thankful that they could be a positive influence in their grandchildren's lives. All expressed how difficult this was for them financially, physically, and emotionally. A few wondered how much longer they could keep up the responsibility before their grandchildren were taken from them and placed in a foster home.

I thought for a few moments about how I would handle this kind of task at my age. I remembered how tiring and difficult it was with my own children when I was much younger. I wondered how many of these fifty-something grandparents, and a few sixty-something ones, ever thought that their lives would turn down this road.

Full-time grandparenting is not really a new phenomenon; it's just becoming more frequent and accepted. Some grandparents who have watched their grandkids being raised in dysfunctional and unhealthy homes have personally launched custody battles for their grandchildren, and won. Others have ended up with grandkids dumped on their front porch in the dead of night.

While they assume responsibility for their grandchildren, these fifty-something people may also have to deal with their children's actions or circumstances that brought about this situation. The problems of abandonment, sexual molestation, incarceration, mental illness, physical abuse, alcohol, drugs, and death don't disappear when children move from the homes of the parents to the grandparents. These struggles merely increase the pressure on the new substitute parents. And many times it is not a two-grandparent team that takes over, but merely a single grandmother or grandfather.

When you find yourself burdened under these new responsibilities, any thoughts of just being "fun" grandparents end abruptly. If you begin to raise a three-year-old granddaughter at fifty-five, you quickly realize that you will be about seventy-two when she finishes college. Grandchildren may keep you young, but being a substitute parent can make you old before *and* after your time.

Many support groups are being formed around the country to assist grandparents caught in this second round of child-rearing. One of the support groups, called

GAP (Grandparents As Parents), is a forum for grandparents to share their struggles, find some positive answers, and stay close to each other. Sessions feature psychologists, social workers, and attorneys who offer professional insights into the grandparents' problems.

The AARP Grandparent Information Center has been set up to help grandparents find the nearest support group or to offer help with questions about custody, health insurance, welfare benefits, or other issues. Call the center at 202-434-2296 weekdays from 9 A.M. to 5 P.M. eastern time.

For the young grandparent of today, there is a nationwide organization called the Young Grandparent Club. Its goal is to help improve relationships between grandparents and grandchildren. For a copy of the club's newsletter, send a self-addressed stamped envelope to: Grandparents' Little Dividends, P.O. Box 11143, Shawnee Mission, Kansas 66207.

Grandparents' Rights. Many grandparents are totally unaware that they even have a voice or any legal rights concerning their grandchildren, but they do. The loss of seeing grandchildren because of their children's divorce or death caused this generation of grandparents to come out fighting for their rights. As a result, since 1965 every state has enacted some kind of legislation addressing grandparents' rights. This does not mean that grandparents have an instant right of visitation. Some of the laws are complicated and the processes are quite involved. If you are uncertain about the laws in your state in this regard, call a family law specialist and talk over your situation.

I believe all children need healthy relationships with

grandparents; children who lose a parent by death or divorce need them all the more. Inner family conflicts and rivalries along with eventual remarriage and blending of families make this a combative and confusing area. Too much of the time, the children become the big losers.

Grandparents As Day-Care Providers

As the American economy struggles and economic realities hit home, many families are looking to the grandparents for day-care. Some families may even move grandparents from distant cities to fill the void. But only very unique grandparents can fit this role. First, they have to live close by and have a home amenable to the responsibility. Second, they must be in good health and have an immeasurable amount of patience. Third, they must love their grandchildren more than their right to be free to pursue their own lifestyle.

Day-care is often a tradeoff. Grandparents get the joy and responsibility of having the grandchildren around while the parents get trusted family members to care for their children. When the children begin school, this burden eases because the grandparents only have the children a few hours in the afternoon. There will be joys and sorrows for all involved, and the species of the carefree retired grandparent may totally disappear.

The grandparents' role is being constantly redefined, but one thing is certain: The nineties will be the decade of more activist grandparents than ever before. An excellent book for in-depth reading in this area is *Grandparenting: Understanding Today's Children* by David Elkind (published by Scott Foresman) and *The Grandmother Book* by Jan Stoop and Betty Southard (published by Thomas Nelson).

Now take a time-out to reconsider your role as a grandparent by finishing the following statements:

So far, as a grandparent, I have

_____

_____

_____

_____

This has been rewarding in the following ways:

_____

_____

_____

_____

After reading this chapter, I think I may have missed some opportunities to expand and enjoy my role as a grandparent. At my earliest opportunity, I am going to:

_____

_____

_____

_____

12

Facing Fifty with Aging Parents

Those who have the most misery in old age tend to be those who have had the least pleasure in being themselves.

Eda LeShan

MY FATHER DIED while I was in college and a lot younger than fifty-something. My mother died five years later—and I was still a long way from fifty-something. I remember the strong feeling I had after my mother died. For the first time I realized I now had no parents on earth and I was very alone. I couldn't call home and just talk anymore. For a long time I felt deserted, even though I hadn't gone home too often when Mother was alive because I had been involved with my own family and responsibilities.

What I think I missed most after they died was the "anchor" that living parents provide for their children. No other anchor ever really replaces the parent. When that one anchor is raised for the final time, you are really on your own, even if you are fifty-something. Until then, just to know your parents are there is a stabilizing thought.

But along with the joy, comfort, and benefits of having our parents with us there are also responsibilities, and as our parents age those responsibilities can resemble those we feel toward our children. In fact, it is not uncommon for fifty-something people to feel like the wishbone being pulled apart after Thanksgiving dinner. On one side are aging parents while on the other are the children and grandchildren. Both may pull at the fifty-something "in-betweeners" with their needs and concerns. At any moment many fifty-something people feel like they will splinter into little pieces—and no one gets a wish!

One force that fuels this delicate balancing act is guilt; we feel we can never really do enough for our parents or our children. And the ultimate need is usually money. Often we don't get the same visible rewards from investing in the care of our aging parents as we get for investing money in our children's future. Still, fifties people want to model adequate love, care, and concern for their aging parents so their own children will one day return the kindness to them. All these pressures can cause fifty-something people to feel a lot of resentment toward both groups, and this can cause family relationships to become fractured and hostile.

In the 1990s these pressures will increase for many of us as older parents are living longer and children are having a more difficult time of establishing themselves financially. Both groups turn to those of us in the middle —just as we may be having our own problems with career and job loss and changing economic lifestyles. Then we end up with the pain of our own circumstances plus the pain of not being able to help the other sides of our family.

Living through our parents' aging and care process may be a time of stress and challenge, but it can also be a time of hope, healing, and care that can send the best message of all to aging parents: *I love you!* Some, like me, wish they still had the opportunity to do this.

What Will We Do with Mother? What Will We Do with Dad?

A lingering part of the American dream is having your parents grow old gracefully with each other in a little white house with a manicured lawn and garden somewhere on Magnolia Avenue. If one dies, the other remains there and is supported by family and friends until his or her death.

Although this dream is lived out for some, it's becoming increasingly rare. Even with increased longevity, older men die much sooner than older women, and the women who remain may struggle with declining health and vanishing finances. When either struggle reaches critical proportions, families start asking the question, "What will we do with Mother (or in some cases, Dad)?"

A classic example of this confusion is revealed in the award-winning film *Driving Miss Daisy*. It is easy to applaud the first part of the film where Miss Daisy is her own person, living contentedly in her own home and taking care of herself. But I shed some tears along with everyone else in the theater when Miss Daisy loses her independence and personhood and is finally confined to a nursing home with sporadic visits from family members.

If aging parents live close by, we can give them some of the care and love they need, but often we are eventually overwhelmed by their growing demands. If they live far away, we can be overtaken by our guilt and inability to be physically present as a source of help, love, and encouragement to them.

Families seldom agree on an answer to the question of what to do with Mom or Dad. The ensuing discussion among the adult children usually brings up the few choices available: your house, my house, or a retirement or nursing home. The hardest questions are:

Who will pay for it?

How will we pay for it?

How will we tell him or her?

How will we convince him or her this is the right decision?

Is this really the right way to go?

What will happen if we make the wrong decision?

If a family is rather large, this decision-making process takes on all the dynamics of a full-scale war, and the "orphan" of this war is the aging parent, who may be allowed little or no say in the final outcome.

Feelings are seldom more strained in any family's life than at this point. What is wise and best is often obscured by feelings of anger, love, confusion, fairness, duty, and guilt.

This was the case when Lucy, the widowed mother of seven adult children, was no longer able to live alone. All of her children except two had scattered to other cities far away from the small town where she and her husband had both been born and where they had reared their children, surrounded by friends and relatives.

At first one of her sons, who was single due to a divorce, moved in to live and care for her. But very quickly Lucy's needs exceeded what he could give.

"I couldn't leave her alone when I had to go to work.

Either she was so ill that she had to stay in bed and then needed help using the bathroom—or she wandered around the house, stumbling over wrinkles in the rug or trying to cook but leaving the burners on. Friends dropped by to see her from time to time, but I could never be sure she was safe whenever she was alone. We tried finding someone to stay with her during the day but either the cost was more than we could pay or the person turned out to be totally unsuitable. Pretty soon it just got to a point where something had to give," the son recalled.

The children met for a family meeting to decide Lucy's fate. The two sons who had remained near Lucy in their home town wanted to put her in a small, rather unsophisticated nursing home there. But one of the daughters described the local nursing home as "an asylum" and said she would "rather die than see Mama in such a place." She wanted to move Lucy to her home in the city, insisting that as a woman and a full-time homemaker she was better trained and accustomed to care for her.

Her siblings argued that Lucy needed to be where her many friends and relatives could visit her, that she would be miserable in such a "far-off place." But the sister prevailed, and without a word from Lucy, her home was sold, most of her possessions were distributed among her children, and she was moved to another state to live with her daughter.

Within two months the daughter, exhausted and frustrated by trying to meet the constant needs of her invalid mother, realized her mistake. Thus, Lucy was moved again, this time to another rather unsophisticated nursing home in the city where the daughter lived. Because she was far from home, only her daughter was able to make regular visits; the other children could come only once or twice a year, and Lucy never saw her hometown friends again. She lived out the remaining six years in what her children came to think of as a warehouse for the living dead.

Lucy's family is not alone in how it responded to this kind of crisis. Throughout the country, wise decisions often go unmade because there is no agreement among all parties involved as to how and where an aging parent will be cared for. A son or daughter may even take a parent into his or her own home to rescue the parent from a family decision he or she did not agree with, as Lucy's daughter did. But a few months later, resentment can build when this adult child fully realizes the obligation and responsibility he or she has undertaken. Meanwhile the aging parent is left to deal with his or her own feelings of rejection, uselessness, anger, loneliness, and lack of love.

In response to this growing trend, organizations and agencies have been set up to assist caregivers in finding the help they need. One of them is the Eldercare Locator, a toll-free telephone service funded by the Agency on Aging; it helps callers locate services for the elderly and their caregivers such as home-delivered meals, transportation, and adult day-care or home care. It also can provide special phone numbers for finding answers to questions about Medicaid, social security, legal services, and other government assistance. Call 800-677-1116.

These services can ease the strain of looking after an elderly parent that, if shouldered alone, can become so intense it leads to abuse or even violence. One horrifying example of the hopelessness that can fill caregivers was lived out in 1991 when a forty-four-year-old Toronto woman shot and killed her eighty-three-year-old mother. After calling to report what she had done, she turned the gun on herself.

Drifting Parents

I watch an increasingly large group of aging parents drifting from one of their children's homes to another. They stay a few weeks or a few months and then move on to the next stop. Some families are happy when they come and even happier when they leave. After a few days, children and grandchildren ignore their needs, wants, and concerns, and isolate them to the guest room for hours at a time. It becomes a duty and obligation for each family to assume the host role for a time. The aging parents feel like intruders and unwelcome guests—gypsies in search of a place to unpack, reside, and really belong.

But these aging drifters may have an advantage over aging parents who move in with an adult child permanently because they're still mobile. Their care demands are less, and their independence is greater. When they run out of family, they can take a cruise or a tour of Europe (if they have the health and finances to do so).

A Mirror of the Future

Aging is a war of feelings and emotions for both fifty-something people and their older parents. When we look at them we see ourselves in twenty years or even less, and this reminds us that their fears will soon become our realities. We become anxious for them as passing years and ill health rob them of the vitality we once took for granted. In turn, they may become jealous of what we still possess and often they unconsciously want us to make them feel vibrant, young, and healthy again. We feel helplessly trapped in our desire to see them as they once were, help them where they are now, or simply push them out of the way and get on with our own lives.

Our feelings often come out in verbal expressions of frustration and anger. If this happens, walls that cut off healthy communication are erected and both sides start distancing themselves from one another. Aging parents look at their adult children and say, "They don't care about me anymore." Fifty-something children respond with, "I don't understand what they want anymore." Patience becomes a rare commodity and estrangement sets in, with potentially deadly results.

How to Keep the Walls Down

There are a number of things we can do to prevent these walls from being erected. Consider how you could use the following eight suggestions to keep your relationship with your aging parents from becoming pained and soured.

1. Both sides need to express their feelings of frustration, anger, or feeling overloaded and over-whelmed *before* relationships become tense. These are real feelings for people on both sides of this relationship, and if they're held in they can easily lead to resentment and bitterness. Then the wall goes up. Most battles are not battles of right and wrong but battles of understanding. Open

communication and honest listening are vital, and the best question to ask is often, "How do you feel about . . . ?" Remember to express your positive feelings as well as the negative ones.

2. Many unkind things are said by aging parents that should not be taken seriously. These things come from their pain, ill health, and advancing age, not from the person we once knew many years ago. Forgiveness should be the order of the day for all conversations centered in negativity and anger.

3. Accept early on that you will never be able to satisfy all the needs, wants, and demands of your older parent. If he or she has spent years of unhappy living, there will be little you can do in the later years to change them into a positive, growing person.

4. Also accept the fact that mental illness is often more difficult to handle in a parent than physical illness. Alzheimer's disease is a real challenge today because the mental acuity goes but the physical body can remain strong for years. We must contend with our human inability to bridge that gap successfully.

5. Set boundaries when dealing with aging parents. Without sane boundaries, you may well be consumed by them. Controllers will still try to control even if they are ninety-nine years old. Aging parents can dredge up years of guilt and send

guided missiles directly to the heart of your fifty-something years.

6. Aging parents generally fall into two common categories: those who insist on remaining independent and will not accept any help you offer and those who are helpless and want you to take care of everything. Be aware that this second response is often used by controllers and co-dependent persons.

7. Honor the histories of your aging parents. Their memories and past experiences give continued meaning to their lives. They are persons who still matter and they need to know they are loved. Talk *with* them, not just *at* them. Don't steal their dignity by treating them like children. This is demeaning and dehumanizing.

8. Make them as much a part of any and all decisions as possible. A sense of worthlessness comes from not being asked about decisions that impact their lives forever.

After reading these eight suggestions, take a minute and write down your responses to the following questions.

Of the eight areas mentioned here, which ones are causing major problems?

_____

Which apply to you but are of only minor concern?

From personal experience in your own life, you probably can add numerous other areas to this list. The dynamics in every family system are different. Some families breeze through any and all problems with everyone appearing to be content and happy. Other families are in constant combat with little resolution on anything. When human dignity is not high on a family agenda, the members, whether young or old, will suffer from loss of self-esteem and self-worth. Older parents are not excepted from this debilitating process and aging only intensifies the damage.

When a Parent Dies

I never expected my parents to die. I also never expected them to live forever in this life. Many people I have talked with expressed the same confusing thoughts. Our problems appear to stem from a "death denial" in our culture, where everything is done to keep us looking, feeling, and acting young. There is no place for a face creased and crinkled by the lines of time in our world unless it's Santa Claus's. We appear to have constructed a generational time line that, when crossed, makes us seem to instantly disappear forever.

Aging in our society could be summed up in one word: *rejection*. Perhaps we subconsciously believe if we reject the aging process, we can also reject the ultimate result, death. How much healthier we would all be if we could talk about it, understand it, and make sane plans for it.

Instead, life insurance salesmen make us more nervous than car salesmen any day of the week. Cemetery plots and markers are for horror movies, not for real life. Terminal illness is never to be talked about until it arrives. Wills and trusts, if drawn up at all, should be written quickly and secretly and locked away in a safe deposit box with the hope that they will never be looked upon again by anyone we know.

Denying a Reality

I have spent my share of time in hospital rooms with dying people, and I have concluded that we don't want loved ones to die not because of what *they* must face, but because of what *we* must face without them. We struggle to keep suffering people on life-support systems for ourselves, not for them. Even when they tell us they are ready to die, we hold on to them even more tightly.

Very few children talk to their parents about death. Fewer talk about the options surrounding death, including keeping the dying person alive indefinitely on a life-support system. Guilt hovers around a decision to cut off the life supports. Those with religious foundations often say it is God's option to take life and ours to try to sustain it. Arguments abound in every corner today. Some people even want the right to take their own life if their disease is terminal and there is no hope of recovery. A Michigan doctor, Jack Kevorkian, has captured national attention in the past months by helping terminally ill patients carry out their wish to die by using a process he has created.

The death of a parent is a place of great change for most people. It not only sharpens the focus on your own mortality but it becomes a personal learning experience.

Dr. Abraham Maslow said, "The most important learnings are internal, intrinsic; one learns more from the death of a parent than from all the academic subjects one studies." Eda LeShan said, "The death of a parent opens up new avenues of insight and perception about dependency, mortality and immortality; the meaning of love and acceptance; the importance of remembering human frailty as well as strength; and the meaning of family and how that includes memories and relationships that suddenly take on new and deeper significance."

The death of a parent can heighten your awareness of how very delicate and precious life is. It can intensify your care and concern about those who are still living and reinforce the reality that they will not always be with you in this life.

The How and When

One of the recurrent fears of death in fifty-something people centers on the "How will I die?" as opposed to the "When will I die?" When a friend dies of a sudden illness such as a heart attack, we respond by saying, "Well, he didn't suffer." When another dies after long suffering, we say, "Well, at least he had time to prepare for it." Death by accident can be labeled senseless while death by old age can be called satisfying.

As we deal with all the issues, feelings, and questions, we can equip ourselves to live with death as acceptable rather than as a denial of life. That does not mean we move into a state of perpetual morbidity; instead we learn to increasingly value our life and the lives of those around us. Saint Paul challenged the early Christians to live life to the fullest and face death with the words, "Where, O

death, is your victory? / Where, O death, is your sting?"
(1 Cor. 15:55).

As a minister, I have conducted many memorial services over the years. Most have been sad, mournful experiences conducted in a sad, mournful atmosphere. I recall
only one that was a celebration of praise at the end of a
life journey. The deceased had requested that it be a
joyful time for he knew where he was going and wanted
others to rejoice that he had arrived. The service included
singing of joyous, promise-filled, up-tempo hymns and
choruses followed by brass instrumental music playing
resurrection-theme hymns. Special, upbeat testimonials
to the deceased were given by family and friends, and
these included more funny stories than sad eulogies. The
pastoral message was filled with hope, praise, and promise. The entire service from church to cemetery exclaimed
a loud *rejoice!* Now that's my kind of celebration! I think I
would like to follow this man's example and give directions for my memorial service while I am alive rather than
have someone else do the guessing after I die.

For Christians, joy and mourning will always be a part
of losing those we love. The sadness is in *our* loss; the joy
is in *their* gain. Fifty-something people with aging parents
have a wonderful opportunity to talk through all this—
including their wishes for memorial services—*before* they
become ill or confined to a rest home. They also have
time to think about their own memorial service someday.

Saying Thank You

One of the things I most regret is that I really never
wrote the one-time, all-consuming, "thank you for everything" letter to my parents. I thought about doing it nu-

merous times, but I never actually did it. I always thought I had plenty of time, but time ran out and the letter in my mind stayed there. Now I am wondering if I will get those kinds of letters somewhere in the future from my own children. Probably not, because they also think they have lots of time.

If your parents are still alive, I want to make a suggestion. Write them that letter. Some of you may be way ahead of me and already have the job done. Others of you may have thought about doing it and just haven't taken the time. *Now* is the time. You may not have a tomorrow.

Some of you may need to do some relational fence-mending with your parents. Unresolved issues often accumulate over the years, dividing children from parents. Some people will never make peace with their past or with their parents and will tearfully cry their regrets in a distant mortuary. You can make a different choice.

Take a time-out right now and think about the things you would include in your thank you letter. The following ideas may help get you started.

1. Thank you for providing a home, food, and clothing. I finally understand how hard that is!
2. Thank you for hauling me all over creation when it was a real inconvenience for you and costly as well.
3. Thank you for your help and encouragement through all my academic years. (And for paying many of those costs.)
4. Thank you for your support and consolation through all my romantic adventures.
5. Thank you for your listening ears and your open heart.

Now add some thank yous of your own:

_____

_____

_____

_____

_____

_____

_____

13

Friends at Fifty

Friendship is the inexpressible comfort of feeling safe with a person having neither to weigh thoughts nor measure words.

George Eliot

IN THE MANY surveys we conducted in preparation for this book, we asked people to list the things that were most important to them as they lived through their fifties. More than 90 percent of them listed family, friends, and God as their top three. Family and God were recognized as the stable, ever-present duo that never changed. Friends were harder to define; they appeared to change frequently and many times were in short supply.

In our fifty-something years, we do not want to spend a great amount of time with just any people. We want to be selective with how we use our time and who we spend it with. But acquiring, keeping, and nurturing friendships is a lifelong challenge for us. Friends enter our lives through usual and unusual experiences, and they often vanish never to return. An unknown author described the friendship process this way: "Our friends float past; we become involved with them; they float on, and we must rely on hearsay or lose track of them completely; they float back again, and we must either renew our friendship . . . catch up to date . . . or find that we don't comprehend each other anymore."

The common ground we all stand on is our need to have friends. Even my favorite comic-strip character, Charlie Brown, frequently says, "I need all the friends I can get." From reading the Peanuts strip, you know that good old Charlie Brown has an odd assortment of friends ranging from Woodstock the bird to Pigpen the filthy. Charlie Brown could be called the ultimate friend to his cast of characters. He is constantly giving and receiving— and being totally perplexed in the process. I readily identify with Charlie and his struggle.

Types of Friends

Our friends usually fall into three different groups. We have casual friends, close friends, and intimate friends.

Casual Friends

Casual friends are best described as the "Hi, how are you? Fine. How are you? See you later! Have a good day," type. Our lives are crammed with casual friends. We recognize them, exchange pleasantries with them, and slip by them. There is little attempt to be anything more to them than we are. They are mostly minor players in the drama of our lives although a few may become major players for a short time if we need something from them.

Close Friends

Close friends are generally the people we socialize with in many areas of life. We can know a lot about them or very little. The focus is more on what we do with them than who they are. They enter our lives through the workplace, our children, the community we live in, or our common interests. They often leave when those dynamics change. The closeness we feel with them can also come from sharing a mutual crisis. Some of life's best friends are made when we go through its deepest points of despair and pain. We become a part of each other's healing and growth when we feel the same things and survive the same experiences.

Intimate Friends

I once read a definition of intimacy that said, "Intimacy involves a willingness to share your hopes, fears, dreams, frustrations, and life with another." It also involves a high level of personal caring, a willingness to risk openness, the ability to be emotionally present to the other person, and a strong commitment to building the relationship over a long period of time. The demands of an intimate friendship will cause most of us to have only a few of these friends at the core of our lives. Some settle for only one. Intimate friends love and accept us as we are with no need or desire to change us.

Intimate friends are generally those we have a history with. That history can go back to childhood, Little League, or elementary school. Or it can be born in college and the post-graduate years and continue through life. It can originate in hospital maternity wards, Girl Scout meetings, PTAs, church choirs, and weekend camping trips.

All friendships start in the casual area, progress to the close level, and may end up in the intimate circle. Most of us pursue friendships more unconsciously than consciously, especially in earlier years, when friendships are taken for granted, used, and discarded. Building a family and career is a priority in the twenty- and thirty-something decades. During those years our friends are people on the edge of our more important things.

But as the years go by, we begin to realize that friends are more important than things, and our priorities change. About the time our children begin to move out of the home, our friendships take on a new and deeper meaning.

The fifty-something decade becomes a sorting place for friendships. Our desire tends to change from wanting to spend time with many people to having richer experiences with a selected few friends. I have personally discovered that I would rather be with old and trusted friends than new and potential friends. I find that I don't have the time or desire to catch the new friends up on the pages of my past life history and begin a new chapter with them. I confess to feeling a little guilty about this from time to time. I know I still must keep a window of my life open to new friends and the definite possibility that God may be sending them to me for special reasons.

Renewing Lost Friendships

In the past few years, I have discovered the value of reconnecting with former friends I had "lost" because of distance, profession, or lack of personal continuity. College friends who were important in my early years have reappeared in my life through unusual circumstances. Although we all continued the mandatory Christmas card or letter each year, there were giant gaps in our history as friends.

Renewing these friendships with people who are also now fifty-something has been rich and rewarding. Hours of talking and exchanging our life experiences have re-united us for the second half of our journey. Distances are no longer barriers to these renewed friendships. We are linked through what we once were to each other, what we have lived, and what we now are equally challenged to become.

Renewed friendships remind us of our past, where we started from, and the progress we all have made. They help us mark our journey through life much as the Israel-ites marked their journey through the wilderness in the Bible.

Several years ago, we had a summer reunion in Florida with a singing group that had been a part of our Youth for Christ ministry back in the late 1960s. Twenty years had passed since this group was last together. They came with spouses, children, and yesterday's memories. It was a time for nostalgia and catching up with lives. When it was over, we left knowing that we had made a difference in the lives of these friends years ago, and we were still important to them and they to us.

Reunions from our academic years can also provide a host of bittersweet memories and new experiences. They are often used to find out how we have faced the storms of life in comparison with our former classmates. Often how we look and what we "do" is more important than that we simply showed up. After the reunion, we can leave feeling we are in better shape than the rest of the old crowd, or we can feel severely depressed because we are in worse condition.

The Impact of Friends

One of the questions I sometimes ask in small groups is, "What person in your life made the greatest impact on you and how?" I used to expect people to name well-known and important people. No one ever did. The names that tumbled out were those of people no one had ever heard of except the people naming them: immediate family members, schoolteachers and youth group leaders, and "ordinary folks." All had given the gift of friendship at a needed time and in a special way. Many people felt impacted by friends who simply gave them time when no one else seemed to care. Others stressed that a friend had really believed in them when no one else did. The sense of being genuinely important to another person was remembered as a wonderful gift. This kind of friendship exemplified love, care, concern, and encouragement. Often it came in the formative years of childhood and was never forgotten.

One fifty-something woman told about the simple gesture of a friend who had come to her home when her father died.

"I was sixteen, and I was totally destroyed by Daddy's death. I felt so alone. The day after he died our house was filled with grieving adults—my parents' friends and my aunts and uncles who had come in from out of town. I had a lot of friends in our small town, and a few of them came with their parents when they made their condolence calls, but they didn't stay long and they seemed anxious to leave. My best friend came with her mother, and as she came in the door I hugged her and started crying. She held me back from her, looked me in the eye, and said, "Let's not think about it. Let's talk about something else. You'll be OK." Of course she thought she was doing the right thing, being strong for me, but at the time that wasn't what I needed.

"She and her mother left in a few minutes and I was alone again in this house full of mournful adults. I know now that my teenage friends just didn't know what to say or do. They were afraid to come to a house in mourning.

"But one friend came. Marcus. I can still see his new Ford Fairlane pulling into the driveway, and in my mind I still watch him walking up to the door, alone. Now I know how brave a sixteen-year-old boy had to be to do that.

"When I opened the door he just stood there, shuffling his feet, not knowing what to say. He finally took a big breath and asked, 'How ya doing?' I shrugged. He said, 'You wanna go for a ride?' Soon we were gliding through the peaceful countryside with the windows rolled down. He let me talk it all out while he just drove, occasionally nodding his head to show me he was listening. He didn't know the 'right' words to say, so he didn't say any. He just let me talk and cry and ride with him. I remember leaning my face out the window and letting the wind blow the tears off my cheeks. It was a tremendous release for me to be with one of my peers who cared enough about me to do this—spend an afternoon with a grieving friend.

"It's been almost forty years since that happened, and I've known a lot of people whose loved ones died. Sometimes I don't want to go to the funeral or to the home; I dread entering the grief-filled room, not knowing what to say. But I always remember Marcus, and I always go."

The Sounds of Friendship

One of our local radio stations held a contest where the listener called the station and tried to identify five every-day sounds that were played. I tried to identify those sounds and couldn't do it, but others could. Why did they know the various sounds and I didn't? I concluded they had listened enough to know them while I apparently did not. We all heard the same sounds every day, but the contest winners listened to the point of recognition.

Our world is filled with sounds. They intrude, distract, frighten, comfort, and interrupt us, creating both a background and foreground for daily living. We accept the sounds of life without even hearing most of them and often ignoring the ones we do hear.

Friends also make sounds. Some are heart sounds while others are head sounds. Heart sounds come from deep within us and draw us close to one another in spirit while head sounds become the verbal expression of what we feel in our hearts. There are six very common sounds that help deepen friendships and move us toward intimacy. I think I have always been aware of them but listening to an audio tape by Rich DeVoss of Amway recently helped me refocus on them.

1. I Was Wrong!

Admitting a wrong is one of the toughest things most of us have to do in a human relationship. We will defend ourselves to our death many times rather than say the simple words, "I was wrong." All through life we struggle to be right because being right brings rewards, accolades, and affirmation while being wrong brings pain, disgrace, judgment, and loss. Right is applauded; wrong is punished. With that indelibly etched upon our brains, who would ever want to say "I was wrong"?

Only those who share a deep level of friendship in our lives will allow us to be wrong without undue judgment and condemnation. Our real friends have learned to love us unconditionally; our friendship with them is not sustained by adding up our rights and wrongs at the end of the month.

Admitting a wrong is therapeutic and releases us from the bondage of perfectionism. Even when we are the only ones who might know, we still need those we are close to to receive our admission of wrong. Most people can handle an admission of wrong better than a denial of wrong.

When you are wrong, admit it and get on with your journey. A person who feels he or she is always right will never have a circle of trusted, intimate friends.

Who in your life today do you need to say "I was wrong" to?

_____

_____

2. I'm Sorry!

Saying "I'm sorry" is generally either a prelude or a postlude to admitting a wrong. It begs for forgiveness from another person. It expresses a deep emotional feeling in the form of a verbal response. Being sorry can emerge from the tritest of all levels, like being sorry for bumping into someone at the mall. Or it can express our deepest desire for the healing power of forgiveness for something we have done to another person or persons. Saying "I'm sorry" is the beginning of rebuilding a relational bridge with another person you have hurt. To be taken seriously, the words must always be followed by some form of action. For many people, however, they are merely words of excuse that precipitate a repeat performance.

Even intimate friends wrong each other at one time or another. There is no perfect friendship. The longer a friendship endures, the easier it is to take each other for granted. Many people feel they can wrong a friend and not say "I'm sorry" because the offender believes the friend understands and accepts him or her after twenty or thirty years of friendship. I believe that the human respect and love we have for one another compels us to admit wrongs and express our sorrow at what we have done.

Over the years I have listened to many stories of people who would never say "I'm sorry," and consequently they lived for years separated from the friends they desperately needed in their lives. Parents and children are often the worst about being too proud to say these words of restoration. Those who travel most successfully through the fifty-something decade have learned to keep short, up-to-date accounts in this area.

Deep friendships are the valuable collectibles of our lives. It's ludicrous to lose longstanding friends over a lack of humility and confession. If we stop to think, there are probably many people we need to call or write to with our personal "I'm sorry" attached. Even when long overdue, these words can help clean out many of the clogged relational arteries in our lives.

Who in your life today do you need to say "I'm sorry" to?

_____

_____

3. I Need You!

What happens when no one needs you? You feel unimportant and uninvolved, and eventually you will suffer from poor self-image and self-worth. We all desperately need to be needed by other human beings. This gives meaning and purpose to our lives.

In Chapter 1 we discussed how hard it is for some of us to say the words "I need . . . " after we have spent a lifetime attending to the needs of others. I admit that for too long I have personally been one of those frontier types who never said, "I need you!" I did not want to bother anyone else, and I felt I was resourceful enough to take care of everything. But I'm not, and you probably are not either.

I realize now that I am in greater need of people at this juncture of my life than ever before. I have also discovered that when I tell someone I need him or her, that person responds by giving me the help I need. Why in the world didn't I discover this years ago? Life would have been so much easier! Maybe it's because in the first half of our lives, *we want to prove things.* And in the second half, *we want to improve things.* We lose many friends in life because that old self-sufficient pioneer spirit still resides within us, haunting us with the words "I can do it myself." They may have worked on the frontier, but they will not work at building a circle of intimate friends.

The wisest fifty-something people have discovered they did not get this far in life without letting a few other people know that they needed them.

Telling people you need them carries a dual impact. It makes the recipients feel worthwhile and important to you, and it tells them they have something positive to contribute to your life. At the same time you are helped, you will be enriched by understanding the feelings the helpers receive from helping you! Both of you will be made to feel special to each other.

How long has it been since you told someone you needed him or her? How long has it been since you were told that you were needed?

Who in your life today do you need to tell "I need you!"?

_____

_____

4. Thank You!

I have traveled in seminar work for the past fifteen years and conducted more than seven hundred seminars. I would guess that I have received fewer than one hundred thank you cards in the wake of this sea of seminars. Were all the participants thankful? Yes! Did they all intend to say so? Probably! Was it really that important to me? Yes, especially when I wondered if I had accomplished anything viable that particular weekend.

"Thank you" is simply expressing appreciation for other people and something they did for you. You are telling them what they did was noted and appreciated, not ignored. Because some people—best friends, parents, spouses, children—are taken for granted, we too often forget to say "Thank you" to them. Or we say it blandly from our lips instead of expressing it meaningfully from our hearts. We may have many friends who have impacted our lives over the years but have never been the recipients of our "Thank yous." Fifty-something is a good time to catch up on that forgotten thank-you list.

Who in your life today do you need to say "thank you" to?

_____

_____

5. *I'm Proud of You!*

I remember when my children first started school. Every day they came home with an armload of finger paintings and drawings. Each one was carefully explained and then stuck on the refrigerator door with tape. When the refrigerator disappeared under all the artwork, the masterpieces went up on the bedroom walls. The artwork was eventually followed by report cards throughout the year. Both were presented to us as parents by the children with the hope of receiving affirmation and acceptance. They wanted us to be proud of them in their accomplishments.

The strongest form of affirmation in the world is to have people say they are proud of you. The opposite extreme is to have people be ashamed of you. The need to receive approval is strong in all of us. Many people live their entire lives in search of an affirming person who will express pride in them. Recognition is a thirst that will seldom be quenched in our lifetimes. One of the strongest sounds we can make in friendship is to tell our friends we are proud of them and proud to be their friends.

Who in your life today do you need to tell "I'm proud of you!"?

_____

_____

6. I Love You!

Of the six sounds of friendship, "I love you" may be the most difficult to express. This is often the one thing that eludes us: being able to look someone in the eye and say, "I love you!" Perhaps we are fearful the response will be "How much?" and we won't be able to think of a good answer. Another part of our hesitation may be that the very word *love* has thousands of meanings, and when we express it to someone, we are never sure he or she understands which meaning we intend. The meaning of love was best expressed by Saint Paul in the thirteenth chapter of First Corinthians, better known as the Love Chapter.

Love can be conditional or unconditional. The world is full of love songs, love poems, and love stories telling us this in phrases such as "love is something you do" and "love isn't love until you give it away."

Fifty-something may be the first decade that love begins to be returned to those of us who have been so freely dispensing it for years. In the last few years, I have noticed that all our children tell us more frequently than ever before that they love us. They have even taught our grandchildren to say "I love you." Maybe this is one unique and rare gift that only comes to those of us in the fifty-something years. (I would have paid money to have our children tell us they loved us when they were teen-agers!)

This may also be the first time many of us who are fifty-something are able to freely say the words, "I love you" to those we need to say it to. Those who have been our friends for the long haul need to hear it. Those who have come lately into our journey need to hear it. We who are free to say it will set others free to say it also.

Who in your life today needs to hear you say, "I love you!"?

_____

_____

Now, look at the names you've written in this section and go tell them, "I'm wrong!" "I'm sorry!" "I need you!" "Thank you!" "I'm proud of you!" "I love you!"

The Spiritual Friend

Many fifty-something people, in their responses to our survey, said they believe their spiritual needs have deepened as the years have passed. I believe that too. Our hunger for spiritual meaning grows more intense in the light of our mortality, and it becomes more important to have spiritual survival skills and tools for the remainder of our life's journey. With these growing needs, it becomes vitally important to be surrounded with special friends who can be a spiritual presence in our lives. They help us continue to develop our spiritual maturity and our spiritual productivity, and they give us a sense of spiritual accountability.

Some fifty-something people have spent a lifetime doing battle with their spiritual windmills without any spiritual friends to help them. Now they are realizing for the first time they need to search for a few friends with a strong spiritual center who will assist them. For those who already have spiritual friends this is a time to draw closer to them, deepening that spiritual bond. One person recently said, "You can quickly evaluate how spiritually strong your friends are by asking yourself which ones you would want standing around your hospital bed praying for you before major surgery."

I have asked many people what they were looking for in a spiritual friend or what characteristics existed in ones they already have. The most frequent response was *the gift of compassion.* This was followed by a number of other qualities, including a presence of the Holy Spirit, a willingness to listen, a certain amount of holiness, plus confidentiality, honesty, kindness, spiritual wisdom, and an ability to really talk to God. Compounded in one person, these attributes would probably only fit Saint Paul, Christ, and a few of the disciples! If we're lucky we will be surrounded by a number of spiritual friends who have these gifts spread among them.

To be a spiritual friend is as important as having one. Spiritual friends share, appreciate, and respond to each other as they are, both humanly and spiritually. We look for the kindred spirits of faith who have fought some spiritual battles, climbed some spiritual mountains, and can join hands with us in our growth and renewal.

I find it increasingly difficult to fit my friends into

many of the spiritual molds I see around me. Too many of them are man-made and not God-designed. I've learned to look for spiritual friends in unsuspecting places where God has planted them. I find some offering their friendship from within the business community while others emerge from service and social groups. Some are estranged from organized churches but are very close to God. God uniquely uses them to be spiritual friends to all who cross their pathway.

A spiritual friend is a person who places one hand in the hand of God and reaches out to you and me with the other one. Perhaps a spiritual friend is best defined by these words of Earnie Larsen, well-known specialist in recovery counseling:

> Thank God,
> thank him a million times over
> for those people,
> those rare, precious, marvelous people
> who have learned the secret place
> and pitched their tents there.
> Those who dwell in the attitudes of
> hope and confidence.
> Who reach across rather
> than down,
> those people
> whose presence
> always leaves us feeling better
> about ourselves.
> Thank God for these
> loving people,
> these custodians of the secret of
> love.

If you are ever tempted to say, "Will my real friends please stand up?" I hope some of those who stand will be spiritual friends.

Be thankful for these people. You are blessed!

14

Living on the Growing Edge

When you are done with doing what's expected of you, you can tap into the incredible power of being yourself.

Karen Blaker,
Celebrating Fifty

WE HAVE ALL seen the sign that says, "Please be patient. God is not finished with me yet!" I would like to add a second part: "And I'm not finished with me yet either!"

If God's work in us is never finished, then our work of continuing to grow should never be finished either. If we choose not to grow, we will wither and die. But if we do choose to grow, we have to risk crawling out onto that growing edge.

Many fifty-something people we spoke to across the country were either worn out by the first half of their lives (therefore desperately in need of a decade of rest) or they felt as if they had just warmed up for the second half (and therefore were ready to hit the fast lane running). We might call them the pooped or the propelled!

Which One Are You?

I have a favorite T-shirt that says, "If you can't run with the big dogs, you better stay on the porch!" I wear it when I am jogging around my neighborhood being chased by Doberman pinschers. The motto on the shirt reminds me I have a choice to run or sit on the porch and watch others run.

But running through life for fifty years can be physically and mentally exhausting. Many people I meet in my counseling have been knocked down, run over, and sidelined by life-draining crises. They are just plain pooped! Dreaming a new dream in their fifty-something years becomes obscured by the past nightmares they have lived through such as divorce, disease, death, career loss, or bankruptcy. It is hard to convince those who are weary from these past struggles that it's never too late for a new beginning in life. Many of them feel they have absorbed all they can from the first half of life and now they want to rock on the porch for the second half.

Dorothy was one example of that. The mother of six children, she had been widowed when she was thirty-two and pregnant. Without even a high-school diploma, she was unable to support her family and soon lost her home through foreclosure. She struggled along by accepting public assistance and by cleaning houses. By the time she was fifty, one of her children had been killed in a car crash and another was in prison for dealing drugs. There was no chance for retirement; there was no money in the bank. And, it seemed, there was no reason to start dreaming at this age.

But Dorothy caught a dream from someone else. Soon after her fiftieth birthday she got a job as an aide in a government-supported child-care center in the inner-city, where she met a woman six years older who was taking evening classes at the local community college. The woman encouraged Dorothy to study for her G.E.D. (general equivalency diploma) and then helped her through the paperwork. Within a year Dorothy and her new mentor were carpooling together to the community college four nights a week. Now Dorothy's dream is to earn a degree in early-childhood education and become a certified teacher at the center where she works as an aide.

Although the schedule is difficult, Dorothy is motivated to succeed. "I look back on what I've been through and I realize this isn't so bad. I've got a good job. And I'm really enjoying learning. I've got a lot of experiences to build on, and somehow that seems to bring the classwork and the discussions into focus for me. I think I can make a difference in this old world by living out my dream, and I know that I can get through the hard parts because I've already had it about as hard as anyone could," she said.

Dorothy switched from being pooped to being propelled. She learned to be a shock absorber who could grow from life experiences that had numbed and disabled her. As one wise person put it, "If we can look at the pain in our lives as being full of potential meaning for the future, . . . then we can say we didn't suffer that experience for nothing."[1] This does not mean you become immune to the shocks that come from living. It means you can reduce their ability to destroy the growth and freedom you desire.

In divorce recovery, I tell people they can either "go through or grow through divorce." Shock waves from any crisis will batter us into submission unless we learn how to absorb them, process them, and move on to greater growth.

Here are some of the ideas I've collected for learning to absorb shock and live on the growing edge of life:

1. Learn to look beyond today and be willing to view tomorrow as a place to rebuild, grow, and learn.
2. Do one positive, growth-producing thing each day.
3. Learn to act on situations rather than react to them. We spend about 70 percent of our time reacting to things when we should be acting on them.
4. Look for ways to bring good things out of bad situations.
5. Don't allow what's already happened to you to prevent you from making positive growth choices in your present or your future.
6. Learn the art of shock absorbing from those who have done it.

By fifty-something, most of us have absorbed a lot of pain and acquired a lot of scar tissue. Many of these scars are on our hearts, invisible to those around us. Seen or unseen, they can become either badges of merit for our victories or signs of defeat that prohibit further growth. Shock absorbers know how to do what my friend Robert Schuller frequently advises: "Turn your scars into stars!"

If your life's journey so far has left you feeling more pooped than propelled, I would like to challenge you to catch a dream, as Dorothy did. Then let that dream lead you to the growing edge of your fifty-something years rather than the rusting edge.

When you live on the growing edge the fifties can be an adventure called "the decade of living dangerously." If you have lived carefully for many years, this change will not come easily. There is tremendous security in the known, while there is grand and glorious insecurity in the unknown. Living on the growing edge is a leap of faith with no safety net beneath you.

In the film *Cocoon* there was a magical swimming pool. When the senior-citizen retirees who lived nearby jumped in, they were filled with vigor, excitement, and new life. The ones who jumped in daily threw caution to the winds while the ones who stayed out asked the swimmers, "Who do you think you are?"

The same thing happens in everyday life. Anyone who steps outside the customary boundaries will be criticized by those who do not. We may even hear the echo, "Why don't you act your age?" The conformers sometimes call it *maturity*. They fail to realize that maturity is not an age; it is a process. It lasts from the beginning of one's life to the end. At no place or time in our journey are we stamped with the word *matured!* (unless it is after we die).

Making Choices That Put Us on the Growing Edge

If someone would have nudged me awake in the middle of my shawl-and-rocker birthday party and asked me what my plan for growth in my fifties was, I would have replied, "To keep living!" Considering the alternative, that would not be such a bad choice!

When I turned fifty I had thought little about locking

on to a stronger growth mode. For a while after turning fifty I felt more haunted by the ghosts of the past than challenged by the options of the present. My physical condition was fine, but my spirit was locked up in the forty-nine-and-holding jail.

One of the greatest gifts God gives any of us is choices. In a democratic society like America, we celebrate our freedom to make choices on the Fourth of July and forget about them the rest of the year, neglecting to implement them in our growth. We fall victim to the easy and the secure, the familiar and the accepted. Our curiosity is sealed in our complacency, and our growth is stunted. To grow is to be fully human and fully alive.

One of our choices is learning to take risks. Lest you miss the point here, let me assure you I am not talking about running out in front of trucks to see if you can avoid getting hit. I am talking about risks that take us out of our cocoon of safety and teach us new and exciting things to enrich our lives.

Taking Risks

Risk-taking involves overcoming a real or assumed danger. Risks must always be evaluated, thought through, and prayed about by those who pray. Trusted friends should be consulted and listened to. Then use the information you gather to decide whether the risk can be taken. That decision always starts with crawling out on the ledge of trust.

Helen Keller said, "Security is mostly superstition. It does not exist in nature nor do the children as a whole experience it. Avoiding danger is no safer in the long run than outright exposure. Life is either a daring adventure or nothing." To this I would add: Risk is not giving up security but strengthening it.

One of the risks at fifty-something is that if we take risks, we may never see sixty-something! Another might be that we will run out of money before we are sixty-something. We could fill several pages with obvious risks that we all face as opposed to those we would choose to run from. The pervading question is, *Will I be a better person by avoiding risks and playing it safe or by taking risks and not having them work out to my own best interest?*

An executive who recently lost a career with a large company told me he was taking a risk he wished he had taken years earlier: He was starting his own business. When I asked how he was feeling about this venture he said, "I'm afraid to do it, but I'm more afraid not to do it."

To be a risk-taker demands that you remember God is still in charge of the universe—and your life as well. The Bible is filled with examples of risk-takers who took a chance on living on the growing edge, like Joseph and Job who had to trust God at their lowest point in life, and their lives were filled with excitement, miracles, and adventure as a result. Joseph went from the pit of despair and the rejection of his family in the desert, to the pinnacle of power over the nation of Egypt. Job, who had everything, lost everything—and then ended his life with more wealth and happiness than he had at his beginning.

Other benefits of risk-taking are expressed in this anonymous poem, which I have been quoting for many years during my workshops:

Risking

To laugh is to risk appearing the fool,
To weep is to risk appearing sentimental.
To reach out for another is to risk involvement.
To expose true feelings is to risk exposing your true
  self.
To place your ideas, your dreams before the crowd is to
  risk their loss.
To love is to risk not being loved in return.
To live is to risk dying.
To hope is to risk despair.
To try is to risk failure.
But risks must be taken, because the greatest hazard in
  life is to risk nothing.
The person who risks nothing, does nothing . . . has
  nothing and is nothing.
He may avoid suffering and sorrow but simply cannot
  learn, feel, change, grow, love, live.
Chained by his certitudes, he is a slave.
He has forfeited freedom.
Only a person who risks is really free!

The process of becoming a risk-taker could be summarized by the eight steps that follow. Consider each one, then complete the statement at the end.

1. Set some goals so you can measure your progress. Then take aim at your goal and keep your focus clear. It was a wise man who said: "Shoot at nothing and that's what you will hit."
   My goals are:

_____

_____

_____

2. Gather information. Ask questions. Prepare for the risks you are about to take. The more research you do, the less the risk factor.
   My questions are:

   _____

   _____

   _____

3. Name your fears about taking this risk and work through them. What is the worst possible thing that can happen as a result of your taking this risk?

   _____

   _____

   _____

   What is the best thing that can happen?

   _____

   _____

   _____

4. Keep your emotions in line when you're taking risks. Don't try to resolve emotions (feeling depressed, angry, vindictive, or hurt) by taking overt risks.
   My present emotions are:

_____

_____

_____

5. Call time-out when you need to evaluate where you are. Risk-taking needs to be looked at periodically from outside the pressure zone.
   I need a time-out because:

   _____

   _____

   _____

6. Take your own risks, not someone else's. If you put your future in the hands of another, he or she controls your fate. *Never surrender leadership in deciding which risks are right for you to take!*
   Who else is currently controlling your future?

   _____

   _____

   _____

7. Decide early in your risk-taking that you will not blame others if your ventures do not work out. President Harry Truman was famous for the sign on his desk that said, "The buck stops here!" Accept responsibility for your actions.

8. Don't expect overnight miracles when you move out on the growing edge and take risks. Thomas

Edison had hundreds of failures before he discovered the incandescent bulb.

When I am introduced before I start a seminar, I sometimes wonder if I am really the person the speaker is describing. I wonder, *Did I do all those things?* As I listen, I decide I like what I hear. It's the description of someone who has been growing and evolving through a half-century of living. I want that process to continue now that I've turned the corner into my second half-century. I want to keep living on the growing edge, even if that edge is getting a little narrower. I will always choose growth and change over safety and comfort. I hope you will too!

We who are fifty-something are now viewing life from the mountaintop. It took a long time for us to climb up here, and now we want to enjoy the view. We have worked hard in raising families and pursuing our careers, and we have experienced both victories and defeats in the pursuit of a meaningful life. We have made a difference, and we will continue to make a difference. Now we want to reach out to those ascending the mountain behind us and inspire them to keep on climbing!

Empowering Others

Before the Olympic Games, thousands of runners carry the torch from Mount Olympus in Greece to the designated site for that year. Each torchbearer has the authority to bear the torch for a few kilometers before passing it on. It arrives at the destination having been *empowered* by each of the bearers.

In athletic terms, to empower means to pass the torch along to someone else and give him or her the authority to carry it. If the decade of fifty-something can be described in many ways, one of them might be "the empowering years." We pass the power of parenting from ourselves to our children (and in return get to enjoy grandchildren without the parenting hassles). We pass leadership in vocation and community to those who are younger (and in return get to begin an avocation, something pursued for enjoyment). We pass on our accumulated wisdom to those who have a desire to learn. We begin to pass on possessions long held in the family to younger members. Fifty-something is a time to end some things, pass on other things, and begin new things.

Living on the growing edge means empowering those around us to do the same, particularly our children. People need to be empowered with trust, love, confidence, self-worth, dignity, honesty, and the knowledge that they are needed.

Empowerment is especially reserved for the human species and contains both tangible and intangible elements. It must emanate from a healthy sense of self, and it is designed for giving away, not for storing up. It is similar to when a teenager gets a set of keys to the family car for the first time. He or she eagerly shows them to everyone, knowing they represent a form of trust and power. However, the keys do little good until they're used to start the car.

Empowerment will keep us living on the growing edge at any age; it needs to be passed from life to life like the Olympic torch is passed from hand to hand.

We empower others by setting them free to make mistakes as well as enjoy success.

We empower others by letting them know we believe

in them, that they are talented and gifted and can accomplish anything they desire.

We empower others by motivating and inspiring them.

To feel empowered, you have to know and believe that the person empowering you is empowered by others. The disciples had no power until they began to follow Christ. Increasingly, His power was given to them, but without Him they were powerless. Ultimately, the disciples were entrusted with full empowerment when they were visited by the Holy Spirit in the Upper Room.

To make this effort easier (and to make us easier to get along with!) here's a prayer that seems to have been especially written for fifty-something people who are *growing older!*

> Lord, Thou knowest I am growing older.
>
> Keep me from becoming talkative
> and possessed with the idea that I must
> express myself on every subject.
>
> Release me from the craving
>   to straighten out everyone's affairs.
>
> Keep me from the recital of endless detail.
> Give me wings to get to the point.
>
> Seal my lips when I am inclined
>   to tell of my aches and pains.
> They are increasing with the years
>   and my love to speak of them
>   grows sweeter as time goes by.

Teach me the glorious lesson that
   occasionally I may be wrong.
Make me thoughtful but not nosey;
   helpful but not bossy.
With my vast store of wisdom and experience
   it does seem a pity not to use it all.
But Thou knowest, Lord, that I want a
   few friends at the end.

Kristone

Postscript

God must have a great sense of humor!

When I began writing about this fifty-something journey, some of the things I was exploring were only happening to others. By the time I finished, about the only things I had personally escaped were death and divorce (mine, that is).

The return of one daughter and two grandchildren to our area has catapulted us into the role of caretaker grandparents. Our once meticulous home now looks like an extension of Toys R Us. We know all the television cartoon characters by first name and we frequently get lost in the mounting avalanche of cookie crumbs that threaten to take over our home.

I am personally exploring a career shift with the accompanying tremors of fear and uncertainty. I alternately want to explore new things or run and hide from *everything*. (I was recently informed that there are no openings at the local monastery.)

The good news is that I soon won't have to face any more of these fifty-something quandaries.

I will soon be sixty-something!

Jim Smoke
Box 24450
Tempe, Arizona 85285

Notes

Chapter 1.   The Fifty-Something Dilemma

1. Cathy Perlmutter with Sharon Stocker, "Self-Help for Midlife Growing Pains," *Prevention*, May 1993, 57.

2. Malcolm Boyd, "Making a fresh start," *Modern Maturity*, February-March 1991, 78.

3. Alan Loy McGinnis, *The Power of Optimism* (New York: Harper & Row, 1990), xiv.

Chapter 3   Still Married after All These Years

1. William H. Bergquist, Elinor Miller Greenberg, and G. Alan Klaum, *In Our Fifties* (San Francisco: Jossey-Bass Publishers, 1993), 82.

Chapter 4   Women: Thriving through the Fifties

1. Eda LeShan, *Oh, to Be 50 Again!* (New York: Times Books, 1992), 60–61.

2. Ibid.

3. Ibid.

Chapter 5   Becoming One's Own Man: Booming in the Fifties

1. Perlmutter, 54.

2. These characteristics based on Ephesians 4:21–24 and Colossians 3:1–11 are included in Leonard LeSourd, "Wild Man or New Man?" *Charisma Magazine*, July 1992.

3. McGinnis, 115.

Chapter 6   Single Again at Fifty-Something

1. David H. Solomon, Elyse Salend, Anna Nolen Rahman, Marie Bolduc Liston, and David B. Reuben, *A Consumer's Guide to Aging* (Baltimore: Johns Hopkins University Press, 1992), 289.

Chapter 8   Beginning Again When a Career Ends

1. Linda Stern, "How to find a job," *Modern Maturity*, June-July 1993, 25.
2. *Ibid.*, 30.
3. *Ibid.*, 34.

Chapter 9   Outsmarting the Retirement Myth

1. John Sanford and George Lough, *What Men Are Like,* quoted in *Catholic World,* November-December 1992, 271.
2. Charles Handy, "Building Smaller Fires: Keep Life Sizzling—Diversify!" *Modern Maturity*, October-November 1991, 35.
3. Adapted from "A day without end," *Psychology Today*, November-December 1992, 11.

Chapter 10   Children Are Forever

1. Alice Rossi, quoted in Winifred Gallagher, "Midlife Myths," *The Atlantic Monthly*, May 1993, 62.
2. Ibid., 60.

Chapter 14   Living on the Growing Edge

1. Kendall Dudley, quoted in "Self-Help for Midlife Growing Pains," *Prevention*, May 1993, 54.